Living Voices

Living Voices

Multicultural Poetry in the Middle School Classroom

Jaime R. Wood

National Council of Teachers of English
1111 W. Kenyon Road, Urbana, Illinois 61801-1096

Manuscript Editor: Lisa McAvoy
Staff Editor: Bonny Graham
Interior Design: Doug Burnett
Cover Design: Diana C. Coe/kō Design Studio

NCTE Stock Number: 30178

Library of Congress Cataloging-in-Publication Data

Wood, Jaime R.
  Living voices : multicultural poetry in the middle school classroom /
Jaime R. Wood.
      p. cm.
  Includes bibliographical references.
  ISBN 0-8141-3017-8 (pbk.)
 1. Poetry—Study and teaching (Middle school)—United States.
2. Multicultural education—United States. I. Title.
  LB1575.W66 2006
  372.64—dc22

                                        2006009577

Permission Acknowledgments

"Cotton Candy on a Rainy Day," "Habits," "Choices," "You Were Gone," "The Rose Bush," "Knoxville, Tennessee," "For Tommy," and "A Poem of Friendship" from *The Selected Poems of Nikki Giovanni* (New York: William Morrow, 1996); "The Funeral of Martin Luther King, Jr." from *Black Feeling, Black Talk, Black Judgement* (New York: William Morrow, 1970) © Nikki Giovanni 1968, 1970, 1972, 1980, 1984, 1996. Reprinted with the permission of Nikki Giovanni.

Li-Young Lee, "The Gift," "Persimmons," "Early in the Morning," "Eating Together," and "Mnemonic" from *Rose*. Copyright © 1986 by Li-Young-Lee. Reprinted with the permission of BOA Editions, Ltd. "Words for Worry" from *Book of My Nights*. Copyright © 2001 by Li-Young-Lee. Reprinted with the permission of BOA Editions, Ltd.

The select poems from Pat Mora are reprinted with permission from the publisher of *Communion, Chants, and Borders* by Pat Mora (Houston: Arte Público Press—University of Houston © 1984, 1991, 1993).

Contents

Acknowledgments

While we tend to think of writing as a solitary act, as one person diligently tapping out words onto a page, ultimately the process of completing this book has been a team effort. Over the past two years, I visited five different schools in or around Fort Collins, Colorado, teaching these lessons and collecting student work. In the end, I think I've learned more from students about how to teach poetry than I will ever be able to teach anyone else. They were candid about what they learned, what confused them, and which lessons were their favorites. For that and all the beautiful experiences I will fold up and slip into my heart pocket, I'd like to thank all of the schools who participated in this project and especially the teachers and students for letting me steal away moments of their class time to do these poetry experiments with them: Boltz Junior High School, Cache La Poudre Junior High School, Colorado State University, Eyestone Elementary School, Lincoln Junior High School, and Pioneer School for Expeditionary Learning.

I might never have started this project without the support of Louann Reid, my advisor and mentor. She is one of those people who guides by example, showing me in countless ways that I could complete this book in the midst of teaching at Colorado State and finishing my master's degree. There were many days when I stopped by her office unannounced to chat about the progress of my writing, or lack thereof, and she not only took the time to read my work and ask difficult questions about my vision, but she was always there. I can honestly say that I couldn't have done it without her.

Lastly, I want to thank my parents, Karen Harmon and Stephen Wood. In her quest to share with me the beauty she finds in the world, my mother read poetry to me from as far back as I can remember, and my father always made me feel as if I could accomplish anything. They are phenomenal people. I can only hope to live up to them.

Introduction

Why Poetry?

For me, that's an easy question to answer. Poetry is my life. It is what I read when nothing else makes sense. It is what I write when I'm trying to make sense of the world. William Wordsworth said that "[p]oetry is the spontaneous overflow of powerful feelings" (Beck 511). Edgar Allan Poe said that poetry is "the rhythmical creation of beauty" (Beck 644). People have been trying to pin down a clear definition for centuries, but one of the wonderful things about poetry is that it cannot be captured in any one lens of understanding. My own definition of poetry is a collection of words without restraint, boundary, or limit; poetry is the necessity that comes from wanting to communicate with the world so badly that all other genres of writing must be abandoned.

While this is what poetry means to me, and countless students and teachers agree with me, this could not be further from how many feel about poetry. *Fearful* and *frustrating* are the words I've often heard to describe the experience that many students have when they read poetry in school. So why teach it? Why put them through such an overwhelming process? Once students get over their fear of poetry, they will find that it can be much less daunting than they originally anticipated. It allows for multiple interpretations of language while still requiring students to support the meanings they construct with textual evidence, which means that there is no one correct answer when it comes to understanding poetry. There are many good answers that allow each student to formulate his or her own interpretation.

Since poetry is generally short, it is easy to focus on details such as word choice, alliteration, and point of view as well as big-picture concepts like symbolism, theme, and cultural studies. Students are able to locate and identify these concepts, which are two of the first steps that are necessary before they go on to understand how these skills are used in literature and eventually how to apply them to their own writing. As you will see in the lessons throughout this book, teachers are encouraged to read the poems multiple times with their students. One of the many benefits of using poetry in the classroom is that it allows readers to examine the text again and again during one class period. Students also have the opportunity to engage in multiple texts in a relatively short period of time, allowing them to collect a vast library of poetry into their repertoire. All of these reasons to teach poetry add up to one overarching goal: to introduce students to a kind of literacy about which they can feel excited. I especially believe that the poetry included in this book has the potential to achieve this goal.

Why This Poetry?

As I taught the lessons in this book, I made a point to ask students what they know about poetry and which poets they have read in school. I received pretty typical answers to both questions: "Poetry rhymes"; "It expresses your feelings"; "It's confusing." Students in every class were able to list Emily Dickinson, Edgar Allan Poe, and Robert Frost, while several students named Walt Whitman, Langston Hughes, and Shakespeare. This is an impressive list, but something about it disturbed me. Out of all of the poets these students remembered, only one is a woman, only one is African American, and none of them is alive. For the first several years of their educations, these students do not ever remember reading any living authors, and they remember few authors with diverse cultural backgrounds. While these authors are important, they are not the only great writers out there. As a matter of fact, there are many poets living right now whose work has the potential to change the way students think about poetry.

The poets presented in this book are all *living voices*. Not only are they all still alive and writing as I lay these words down, but they all have cultural backgrounds that parallel many of the lives of our students. Nikki Giovanni is an African American woman who teaches in the English Department at Virginia Polytechnic University; Li-Young Lee is a Chinese American man who lives in Chicago with his family; and Pat Mora is a Latina native of El Paso, Texas. I remember finishing the unit on Nikki Giovanni and telling my students about how I had interviewed her a few months earlier. I was able to describe what she looks like, how she talks, and what an amazing presence she has. I gave my students the address to her Web site and told them that they could hear her read her own words there and that she has been known to visit middle schools. They looked at each other and smiled at the possibility of a famous poet stopping into their class to say hello. Li-Young Lee and Pat Mora both travel around the United States speaking about poetry at universities, and Mora has been known to visit schools and lead writing retreats for teachers. These writers can become real people for students. Students feel physically closer to them because they are alive and because these poets offer a new mirror for students to look into. Students who are only exposed to the previously mentioned authors are seeing a very limited picture of the world and, more important, of themselves. As Adrienne Rich said,

> When those who have the power to name and to socially construct reality choose not to see or hear you, whether you are dark-skinned, old, disabled, female, or you speak with a different accent or dialect than theirs, when someone with the authority of a teacher, say, describes the world and you are not in it, there is a moment of psychic disequilibrium, as if you looked into a mirror and saw nothing. (199)

I truly believe that one of the greatest responsibilities of teachers is to provide students with as many positive mirrors as possible. One way to do this is to help them get to know a variety of authors in depth.

How Should You Use this Book?

How you use this book will depend upon what you want to focus on. If you want students to become familiar with the authors in this book as you teach the concepts, you will probably want to stick with teaching chapter by chapter. When I began writing this book, I decided to organize the chapters by author rather than by topic because I visualized students spending a few days or more focusing on each author before moving on to the next. I still think that would be a valuable way to use this book, but it's definitely not the only way. The advantage of studying one author at a time is that students can really get to know each poet, creating a greater opportunity to make lasting connections. When the book is taught one chapter at a time, students can learn about each poet's style of poetry, the subjects each one focuses on, and who they are as people.

Another way to use this book is to combine lessons from different chapters that teach related topics. For example, in Chapter 1, two of Nikki Giovanni's poems are used to teach simile and symbolism, and in Chapter 2, Li-Young Lee's poetry is used to teach metaphor. Since these are all similar concepts, it makes sense to teach them together. There are several places where lessons from different chapters seem to overlap in that way, which makes it easy to move to and from different chapters seamlessly.

This book might also be used as a part of units that are already taught as part of your curriculum. For example, when I taught the Nikki Giovanni section in Chapter 4, students were studying the history of African Americans from slavery to the present. Having students learn Dr. Martin Luther King Jr.'s "I Have a Dream" speech was a powerful way to incorporate my lesson into the unit that was already being taught. Integrating poetry into other subject areas is a powerful way to make even more connections, not only between the students and the poetry, but also between different disciplines. Chapter 4 is devoted to demonstrating the different ways poetry can be used across the curriculum.

Of course, for those of you who just want to see how your students react to this poetry, I suggest opening *Living Voices* at any lesson and jumping in. While the lessons work well when taught together, each lesson can stand alone. Many of the lessons have been tested in a variety of school settings, ranging from a rural sixth-grade classroom to a seventh-grade classroom in an expeditionary-learning outward-bound school to an eighth-grade classroom in a junior high school with a large population of students whose second language is English. In some situations, I was able to teach the book from one chapter to the next, whereas other classes required that I work my lessons into their curriculum. In these cases, I taught lessons that built on what students were already learning. No matter where I tried these lessons, students came away from them better able to talk and write about poetry.

Throughout the content chapters, you will find charts and diagrams I use in the classroom to help students work with various elements of poetry. Feel free to photocopy the blank versions of these forms in the appendix to use with your own students.

I encourage teachers in grades 6 through 12 to share the poetry in this book with your students any chance you get, regardless of what subject you teach. Poetry can be a powerful literacy tool, and an engaging way to connect students to new learning experiences. Most important, I hope that students and teachers can learn that poetry is more than just a passing frustration; it can be a passion that carries on in the lives of students long after they leave our classrooms.

A Little about Me

I am a teacher. I believe that all people are; a few of us just decide to teach in a classroom instead of out in the world. I've been working with school-age children for close to ten years in different capacities, but much of my formal teaching experience has come in the past three years. In 2001, I was hired to help start Pioneer School, the first expeditionary-learning outward-bound school in northern Colorado. My experience at that school provided the foundation for what I've created in *Living Voices*. Besides writing and mapping curriculum and planning interdisciplinary lessons with a team of teachers, I was also asked to combine classroom learning, fieldwork, adventure trips, and service learning into meaningful, connected experiences. All of this was accomplished without using textbooks or evaluating with grades. Based on my experiences at Pioneer, I strongly believe in constructivist education, the idea that students have the capacity to discover knowledge in their own unique ways with our guidance.

This philosophy of teaching is beautiful because students are not so much being fed meals of information cooked up by someone else, so to speak. Instead, they are constructing something new based on the ingredients they already have without necessarily knowing what all of the ingredients are or what the meal is to be called until afterwards. For example, in Chapter 3, students are asked to use sensory language to describe known objects in new ways. When they begin, they have no idea that the meal they are preparing is called sensory imagery, or that this activity is practice in order to identify and explain the importance of sensory images in one of Pat Mora's poems, which is ultimately the goal of the lesson. All of this is done without defining concepts for students because they come to the definitions themselves through exploration and questioning, and therefore they are feeding themselves new knowledge that is more appetizing than information that is fed to them by someone else. Not only are constructivist methods more successful for students, but I have found that I am a more satisfied teacher when I organize my lessons this way. My relationship with students becomes a collaboration in which students show me what they know, and I show them how they can use the knowledge they already have to learn new things.

I am also a poet. Writing has been part of my life since I was a young child and my mother bought me my first journal. I wrote in it nightly and always imagined writing something that other people might want to read some day. Since then, I have self-published a chapbook of forty-three of my poems and have sold close to one hundred copies of the book. I have also had three poems published in different literary journals and magazines. I have been writing for nearly twenty years, which gives me an intimate understanding of what it takes to write, read, and understand poetry. *Living Voices* is a reflection of this understanding. It integrates reading and writing, with a focus on reading comprehension and making personal connections to poetry.

Above all else, my hope is that the teachers and students who experience the poetry in this book discover a passion for language that will linger, that will become a transforming part of their lives. Enjoy!

1 Nikki Giovanni

I remember sitting as a child with my mother—I couldn't have been more than seven or eight—listening to her read poetry. She helped me memorize Blake's "The Chimney Sweeper" and dream about Wordsworth's daffodils. But there was one voice, one piercing rhythm, that I remember above everyone else's. It was Nikki Giovanni's.

Cotton Candy on a Rainy Day

Don't look now
I'm fading away
Into the gray of my mornings
Or the blues of every night

Is it that my nails
    keep breaking
Or maybe the corn
    on my second little piggy
Things keep popping out
    on my face
      or
    of my life

It seems no matter how
I try I become more difficult
    to hold
I am not an easy woman
    to want

They have asked
    the psychiatrists   psychologists   politicians and
    social workers
What this decade will be
    known for
There is no doubt   it is
    loneliness

If loneliness were a grape
    the wine would be vintage
If it were a wood
    the furniture would be mahogany
But since it is life   it is
    Cotton Candy
      on a rainy day
The sweet soft essence
    of possibility
Never quite maturing

I have prided myself
On being in that great tradition
   albeit circus
That the show must go on
Though in my community the vernacular is
   One Monkey Don't Stop the Show

We all line up
   at some midway point
To thread our way through
   the boredom and futility
Looking for the blue ribbon and gold medal

Mostly these are seen as food labels

We are consumed by people who sing
   the same old song   STAY:

                        as sweet as you are
                        in my corner
Or perhaps   *just a little bit longer*
But whatever you do   *don't change baby baby don't change*
Something needs to change
Everything   some say   will change
I need a change
   of pace   face   attitude and life
Though I long for my loneliness
I know I need something
Or someone
Or. . . . .

I strangle my words as easily as I do my tears
I stifle my screams as frequently as I flash my smile
   it means nothing
I am cotton candy on a rainy day
   the unrealized dream of an idea unborn

I share with the painters the desire
To put a three-dimensional picture
On a one-dimensional surface

The emotion, the words so real that I understood them from the inside out, created a love for Nikki Giovanni's poetry that has been with me ever since. She has the ability to take words that we use every day and turn them into awe-inspiring poetry.

When I decided to become a teacher, I knew that sharing my enthusiasm for poetry with students needed to be a priority. I wanted it to be in my classroom all the time, but students did not always respond well to poetry. Through past experience or lack thereof, they had learned that poetry was intimidating; it didn't make sense. Nikki Giovanni's poetry is different. It is easily accessible both because of the language she uses and the subjects she explores. This is especially important when engaging middle school students with new poetry. They have to be able to relate to it personally, to feel as if the poet is speaking to them.

In the following chapter, I present several teaching ideas that can be used to acquaint middle school students with Nikki Giovanni's poetry while also teaching important language arts concepts. I teach poetry to instill a love for it, to help students understand it so thoroughly that it will stick with them beyond my classroom walls, and to promote literacy in ways traditional textbooks cannot. By becoming immersed in Nikki Giovanni's poetry, students will have the opportunity to form relationships with her as a writer and as a person.

Listening to the Speaker

When students read poetry that uses first-person "I," they often assume that the author is talking about herself. While that may be true, it is important for students to be aware of the possibility that the author has chosen to use "I" to write about someone else. Sometimes poets use the first person to sway readers to think of themselves while they read. Poets may also do this to place themselves within situations that they have been affected by but have not experienced firsthand. Then again, sometimes the poet *is* making an autobiographical statement.

Prereading: Making Personal Connections

Before doing the prereading activity, make sure students understand what point of view is so that they can identify first-, second-, and third-person points of view. They will need this information as they do their own writing.

Write the words *habits* and *choices* on the board and ask students to choose one of them to write about. Give the students a number, either a one or a two, and tell them that all the ones are going to write about their word from their own point of view. All of the twos are going to write from someone else's point of view, but everyone must use first-person "I" in their writing. "How can we use 'I' to write about someone else's habits or choices?" they may ask. Simple: they must step into someone else's shoes and speak as that person. Some students may want to start with a specific person and a specific habit or choice in mind to help them get a better sense of whose voice they are using. The goal is for students to produce a paragraph or a poem describing how habits or choices have affected their or someone else's life.

Once they have written their descriptions, ask a few ones and twos to share with the class.

Habits
Marie

I used to have bad habits. Like when I was younger I used to chew my nails. My incentive to stop was I would get my ears pierced. Not chewing my nails was really hard for me and it took me a couple years. I also had to get glasses. At first I was so excited about them I wore them all the time, but as the years went by I became less excited and I would forget them. Habits are hard to break, but they are also hard to remember.

Choices
Zenna

Bad things have happened
within and amongst our friends
I don't want to be a part of it
so this is where it ends

I'm leaving to go out on my own
and leave the clique behind
to start out completely fresh and new
and ease my troubled mind

I'm leaving now to say goodbye
to leave the chaos behind
you may choose to leave with me,
to tell the trouble "goodbye"

Now, open up the class for discussion about how it feels to use "I" when writing from someone else's point of view and how its meaning changes when it is used to talk about the author. Ask students to explain why an author might use first person for different reasons, and write their responses on the board. Keep this list to be used after students have read the two poems.

Classroom Snapshot: Below are some of the ideas my students had about point of view.

- It's easier because you don't have to think so much about yourself and you can observe things about other people. You don't have to worry so much about how you're going to portray yourself. (Patricia)

- Sometimes it's better than third person because some people don't want things written about them so to write about them you can just write in first person. (Hali)

- If you're writing about someone who's not real. (Charles)
- It's a way to write about who you want to be. (Ann)
- It gives more feeling and helps you get over something. (Ileana)

Reading

This section focuses on two poems, "Habits" and "Choices," to introduce students to the idea that the speaker and the poet may or may not be the same person. Read both poems aloud to the students twice. The first time, students should read along to become familiar with the poems. The second time, ask students to underline any words or phrases that may give a clue as to who the speaker is. Since some students are unable to work while someone is talking or reading, give the class a few minutes to read both of the poems on their own to collect as much information about the speakers as possible. It is also a good idea to take the time to make sure students understand all of the language in the poems. "Choices," for example, uses the word *lateral*, which may be unfamiliar for some students.

In the first poem, the speaker laments over the habit of loving too much. It isn't clear whether the speaker is a man or a woman, which makes this a good poem to start with when introducing Giovanni's poetry to students.

Habits

i haven't written a poem in so long
i may have forgotten how
unless writing a poem
is like riding a bike
or swimming upstream
or loving you
it may be a habit that once acquired
is never lost

but you say i'm foolish
of course you love me
but being loved of course
is not the same as being loved because
or being loved despite
or being loved

if you love me why
do i feel so lonely
and why do i always wake up alone
and why am i practicing
not having you to love
i never loved you that way

if being loved by you is accepting always
   getting the worst
   taking the least
   hearing the excuse
and never being called when you say you will
then it's a habit
like smoking cigarettes
or brushing my teeth when i awake
something i do without
thinking
but something without
which i could just as well do

most habits occur
because of laziness
we overdrink
because our friends do
we overeat
because our parents think
we need more flesh
on the bones
and perhaps my worst habit
is overloving
and like most who live
to excess
i will be broken
in two
by my unwillingness
to control my feelings

but i sit writing
a poem
about my habits
which while it's not
a great poem
is mine
and some habits
like smiling at children
or giving a seat to an old person
should stay
if for no other reason
than their civilizing
influence

which is the ultimate
habit
i need
to acquire

The second poem is about the struggle to feel satisfied even when your choices are limited. Middle school students are overly familiar with the notion of not having as much choice as they would like, so they are easily able to relate to this poem. Again, the speaker's identity is ambiguous. Readers are invited into the speaker's emotions, but never get to know this person from the outside, which, of course, is done for a reason. This poem provides an opportunity for students to discuss the rationale for using "I" and how its use affects their understanding of the poem.

Choices

if i can't do
what i want to do
then my job is to not
do what i don't want
to do

it's not the same thing
but it's the best i can
do

if i can't have
what i want   then
my job is to want
what i've got
and be satisfied
that at least there
is something more
to want

since i can't go
where i need
to go   then i must   go
where the signs point
though always understanding
parallel movement
isn't lateral

when i can't express
what i really feel
i practice feeling
what i can express
and none of it is equal
i know
but that's why mankind
alone among the mammals
learns to cry

After reading each poem, ask students to share their opinions of the poems in general. This can serve as a preassessment of their understanding of the poem's basic message as well as a gauge for what they think about the speaker.

Classroom Snapshot: When I discussed the speaker of "Habits" with my students, we had a rather heated conversation about why the speaker was either a man or a woman. I was shocked and excited to witness them questioning gender roles so adamantly. As one boy argued that "boys don't talk like that," a group of girls protested that they hear guys talk that way all the time, and another boy disputed that guys can express emotion as much as girls can. I taught this lesson with four different classes, and all of them had the same type of debate when I asked them to give textual evidence to support their answers.

Activity: Using Textual Evidence

Put students into groups of two or three to create descriptions of the speakers in these poems. They must start out by explaining who the speakers are in detail. Give each group a three-column chart, like the one in Figure 1.1, and ask them to answer the questions. Once the groups have answered these questions, have them find evidence from the poems to support their answers. The evidence should be written in the right column of the chart.

Give each group a chance to present their charts to the class, and encourage the class to ask questions of each group as it presents. As groups present their answers, the class will challenge them to clarify why a certain passage from one of the poems made students think the author was young or male. This will require students to think critically about the answers they give and the evidence they find.

Extensions

Getting to Know the Author

After this exercise is a perfect time to give students some background information on Nikki Giovanni. If time is short, give students a fact sheet on the author, but otherwise turn the search for information into a scavenger hunt. Give students a list of facts they must find about Giovanni,

Identifying the Speaker

Directions: In the middle column answer the questions about the speakers. Use the right column to give evidence from the poem to support your answer.

Questions	Answers	Textual Evidence
Are the speakers male or female? "Habits"	Female	"if you love me why/do i feel so lonely"
"Choices"	Male	"i can't express/what I really feel"
What activities do these speakers participate in? "Habits"	Smoking, drinking, overeating	She listed all these things in the poem.
"Choices"	Wanting to get her way.	"if i can't do/what i want to do/then my job is to not/do what i don't want/to do."
How old are they? "Habits"	20's	Because of the drinking and smoking
"Choices"	Teens	She speaks like a teen in this poem, especially in stanzas one, three, and four.
How do they feel in these poems? "Habits"	Rejected	The whole third stanza
"Choices"	Misunderstood	"when I can't express/ what i really feel/i practice feeling/what i can express"
What from the poems relates to you? "Habits"	Yes, feeling like the guy I like doesn't like me back.	"if being loved by you is accepting always/getting the worst/taking the least/hearing the excuse"
"Choices"	Standing up for what you think is right	"when i can't express/ what i really feel/i practice feeling/what i can express"

Figure 1.1. Student answers.

and turn them loose in the computer lab or library. Below is a list of interesting facts about Nikki Giovanni. Note: This list can be used again in the Nikki Giovanni section of Chapter 4 when students will need to know who Giovanni is as a person in order to successfully complete the reflective writing exercises.

- She was born Yolande Cornelia Giovanni Jr. in Knoxville, Tennessee, on June 7, 1943.
- When she was little, her sister, Gary, started calling her Nikki, and the name stuck.
- She was raised in the Cincinnati, Ohio, area until she reached the tenth grade when she went back to Knoxville to live with her grandparents.
- In 1967, Nikki finished her bachelor's degree in history and became actively involved in the Black Arts movement.
- Giovanni published her first book, *Black Feeling Black Talk*, in 1968 at the age of twenty-five.
- In 1968, she entered Columbia University to study creative writing and dropped out after someone in the creative writing department told her she couldn't write.
- She went to Martin Luther King Jr.'s funeral in Atlanta, Georgia, in April of 1968.
- In 1969, she gave birth to her only child, Thomas Watson Giovanni.
- At the age of thirty, she won the Woman of the Year award from the *Ladies' Home Journal*.
- Giovanni became a Full Professor of English at Virginia Tech in 1989, where she still teaches today.
- In 1995, she was diagnosed with lung cancer. She went through surgery to remove it and is currently healthy.
- Since 1972, she has received twenty-two honorary doctorates for her achievements in poetry.
- Nikki Giovanni has written eighteen books of poetry, six of which are for children. She has made nine recordings of her poetry and one film called *Spirit to Spirit*.
- To learn more about Nikki Giovanni's life, go to her timeline page at http://69.65.21.121/~nikkigi/timeline.shtml.

Comparing and Contrasting

Now that students know a little about the author, they may have different ideas about who the speakers are in the poems. Using the Venn diagram in Figure 1.2, have students compare and contrast the speak-

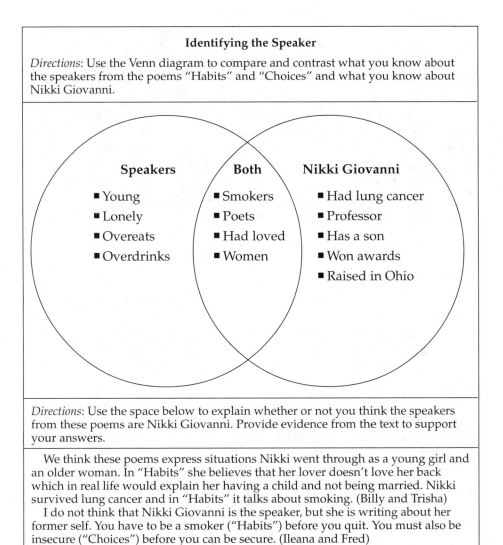

Figure 1.2. Student answers.

ers in the poems with Nikki Giovanni. Ask them if they think she is the speaker in these poems. They must provide evidence from the text to support their answers.

Classroom Snapshot: Not only did my students learn quite a bit about Nikki Giovanni by trying to understand who the speaker might be in these poems, but they also gained a whole new perspective about how to interpret poetry. When students read poetry, it is important for them to ask themselves questions about the speaker that will give them greater insight into the poem. From what perspective is this person speaking? How do I know? How does this perspective affect the meaning of the poem? How does it affect the way I relate to the poem? As students start to learn that it is dangerous to make assumptions about poetry, they will learn to delve deeper into each line in order to find meaning.

Recognizing Literary Technique

"Why do I need to know this?" "When am I ever going to use this?" I've heard these questions more than once from my students. They often have trouble seeing the benefit of what they are being asked to learn, especially when they are in middle school. Many middle school students are stuck without the enthusiasm they had in elementary school and without the graduation light at the end of the tunnel. When they ask such questions, it should be translated as, "If you can't make this relevant, I'm going to tune you out." They need to see how it will help them or relate to their immediate lives. So how is this done when you're teaching literary techniques like simile and symbolism? This chapter includes two of Nikki Giovanni's poems and explains how they can be used to teach simile and symbolism in a relevant, creative way.

Prereading: Creating Similes

Begin by having a conversation about what similes are. Then give students the following list, or one like it, and ask them to work individually to add similes that make the sentences more descriptive:

- They are watching. (How are they watching?)
- I am sick. (How sick are you?)
- The car is fast. (How fast is the car?)
- The house was dark. (How dark was the house?)
- Chores are forgotten. (How are chores forgotten?)

When they finish, have several students share their modified sentences, and discuss the difference between the sentences with similes and those without.

> They are watching like an eagle that has spotted prey. (Alex)
> They are watching as close as a tiger ready to pounce. (Xyla)
>
> I am as sick as a mouse who ate poison. (Wes)
> I am sick like a weed that was sprayed with pesticide. (Nicole)
>
> The car is as fast as lightning. (Patrick)
> The car is as fast as a gazelle. (Marshall)
>
> The house was dark like a rabbit hole. (Jenny)
> The house was as dark as the midnight sky. (Alana)
>
> Chores are forgotten like homework. (Paul)
> Chores are forgotten as if they were old socks. (Grace)

Classroom Snapshot: I wanted students to think about why they might ever use similes in their writing or speaking, so I asked them to explain why the sentences were better with similes than they were without them. They said that the new sentences were more interesting because "they paint a picture in your mind," as one student explained, and because they were more specific and detailed. It is important to discuss *why* literary devices such as similes are better than less descriptive writing instead of just expecting students to believe it. Once they verbalize the idea that their writing might have been less interesting without these tools, students are more likely to add them to their writing repertoire.

Another way to begin this activity is to give students a list of objects (car, tree, house, bird, etc.) and ask them to choose one to draw. Once they have drawn their object using as much detail as possible, have them pass their drawings to a neighbor. The neighbor must write a sentence that describes the picture using similes. If a student drew a red sports car, for example, the neighbor might write something like, "The red sports car zooms past the stop sign like a wild fire racing through the forest."

Reading

To introduce the poem, write the phrase "You were gone" on the board and ask students to explain what the phrase means, listing their answers on the board. The point of beginning this way is to show students how many interpretations these three words can have when they stand alone. There is no way of knowing who the "you" is or where the person has gone. They may have taken a drive or they might have died; there is no way to know, but the similes that Nikki Giovanni adds in her poem help to clarify her meaning.

You Were Gone

You were gone
    like a fly lighting
    on that wall
    with a spider in the corner
You were gone
    like last week's paycheck
    for this week's bills
You were gone
    like the years between
    twenty-five and thirty
    as if somehow
You never existed
    and if it wouldn't be
    for the gray hairs
    I'd never know that
You had come

Classroom Snapshot: When discussing the use of similes in this poem, I asked students to compare the list on the board with the similes Giovanni uses in the poem. How do her similes change the meaning of the phrase, "You were gone?" What tone does the poem have due to the use of similes? My students decided that it was much easier to determine who Giovanni was writing about and what the speaker's relationship was to this person after adding the similes. They believed that the person who was gone was special to the speaker because of the dramatic nature of the similes Giovanni used. They also thought that this was a person the speaker worried about because of the gray hairs that are mentioned at the end of the poem.

After discussing the similes, ask students to manipulate some of them. Play with the poem by turning some of the ideas listed on the board into similes and replacing Giovanni's similes with the new ones. One way to do this is to put the poem on an overhead with the similes removed, leaving space to write in new ones. Give students a chance to come up to the overhead to write in one of the similes they like from the board. Discuss how the tone of the poem changes, as well as the meaning, as the similes change.

You Were Gone
Class version

You were gone
    like an eagle
    that had spotted
    prey
You were gone
    like a lost dog
You were gone
    like homework

The similes used in the class version of "You Were Gone" range from violent (an eagle spotting prey) to playful (lost or forgotten homework), which changes the tone from Nikki Giovanni's version. Her similes focus on adult issues (bills and growing old) and things that can never be returned (money already spent). This causes the tone of her poem to be more regretful while the similes in the class poem work to give it a feeling of powerlessness. Just by playing with the similes, students were able to alter the tone of the poem to better fit their perspective on what it feels like to lose something.

Extension

Simile Poems

Have students use the first line of the poem, "You were gone," to write group poems using similes. Start by putting students into groups of four, and ask them to think of something that they have all lost or a person who is gone from their lives that they would be willing to write about. Students can use the form of Giovanni's poem as a guide. Each student in each group will write one simile for the subject that their group has chosen. Then, each group will combine their four similes, deciding what order to put them in to create a poem of their own. Students can also work individually and choose a completely different subject to write simile poems using Giovanni's poem as a guide.

You Were Gone
Grace, Rusty, Alex, Larry

You were gone
 like whisked
 away leaves
 in the wind
You were gone
 like a tear
 in the ocean
You were gone
 like a lightning
 bolt out of
 the clouds
You were gone
 like childhood
 memories when
 you're old

Oblivion
Nicolas

you fell into Oblivion
 like a candle,
 burning vibrantly,
 then choking
 on its own wax.
you fell into Oblivion
 like a moth trapped
 in a web and the
 more moving it does
 the tighter the snare
 gets.
you fell into Oblivion
 as suddenly as an
 owl swiftly silently
 slays its prey.
and the only thing that
 brought you back
 was Love like
 a shield saves
 a man from war.

Symbolism

Symbolism is a difficult notion for middle school students to comprehend, but it can be done if the concept is made concrete. Begin by talking about public symbols, those symbols that we see in our world ev-

ery day, and then move on to literary symbols, those objects in literature that represent something greater than the literal thing.

Give students a list like the one below and ask them to explain
what each thing stands for. Discuss the meaning behind each of these
concrete symbols. What is the difference between their literal meanings
and their figurative meanings? How is the cultural meaning assigned?
How do all of us know what these things stand for?

- Wedding ring (union, eternal love, fidelity, binding of two
  people in marriage)
- The Golden Arches (McDonalds, fast food, cheap food, ham-
  burgers, French fries)
- The Nike symbol (expensive shoes and clothing, sports, Ro-
  man symbol for victory)

Now ask students to think of concrete things that they see in their
daily lives that may be symbols for something else, and have them make
a list of at least five such objects using the Symbolic World chart in Figure 1.3. As they complete this chart, they will also describe the objects
both literally and figuratively. When students have completed this task,
ask for volunteers to share. (See Figure 1.3 for student answers.)

Reading: Application

Read the poem aloud to the class, and have them read along silently.
During this first reading, students may mark any words or phrases that
interest them. Then go back and read the poem again, asking students
to only mark things in the poem that could be symbolic. Have students
use their charts to record the things from the poem that they marked.
Give them a few minutes to write down what they think the literal and
symbolic meaning of each thing is. Then open up the class for discussion about the different symbols in the poem and what the poem might
mean. Keep in mind that it is okay and even good for students to give
multiple readings of a poem, but they must be able to explain their readings using textual evidence.

The Rose Bush
(for Gordon)

i know i haven't grown but
i don't fit beneath the rose
bush by my grandmother's porch

i couldn't have grown so much though
i don't see why the back of the couch
doesn't hide me from my sister

the lightning that would flash
on summer days brought shouts
of you children be still   the lightning's
gonna get you

we laughed my cousins and sister and i
at the foolish old people
and their backward superstitions
though lightning struck me
in new york city
and i ran
to or from what   i'm not sure
but i was hit
and now i don't fit
beneath the rose bushes
anymore
anyway   they're gone

Extension

Write to Learn

Ask students to write a paragraph, story, or poem describing the first time they realized they were growing. They should think of something that would symbolize their growth the way Giovanni did in her poem. They might want to brainstorm a list of objects that helped them realize they were growing and changing and decide how those objects might be symbolic of that change.

"The Journal"
Kasey

Just last week I was reading in my little sister's journal. In the journal, she mentioned how she was bored and how she could not play with me because I was with friends or doing homework or babysitting. She said that we don't really get any sister time anymore. While reading this journal and experiencing childhood again through her eyes—how she raced her friend at recess, how she tried desperately to climb a tree to the very top in order to peek into a bird's nest, how she helped to rescue a little caterpillar who was going to get trampled by feet—I began to realize how fast my childhood has gone away. I used to climb trees. I used to rescue animals and play with insects. I used to try to keep myself awake until the next morning. It was after reading my sister's journal that I realized how much I missed it.

The Symbolic World

Directions: Use the left column to list five objects from your daily life that have symbolic meaning. In the middle column, briefly describe what the object is literally. Explain what the object means symbolically in the right column.

Object	Literal Meaning	Symbolic Meaning
Money	Paper with designs on it	Power and wealth
Uncle Sam	A man pointing at you	The U.S. wants you to join the army.
Ying-Yang	A circle with squiggly lines and two dots	It symbolizes balance.
Ballet shoes	Cloth and leather	Support, pain, and elegance
Light bulb	Glass and metal	Hope or a bright idea.

Directions: Use the space below to record all of the things in the poem "The Rose Bush" that have symbolic meaning.

Object	Literal Meaning	Symbolic Meaning
Rose bush	A plant with leaves and flowers	Getting older
Lightning	Electricity in the sky	Change and fear
Couch	A piece of furniture	Safety and games
New York City	A big city in America with lots of buildings and people	Adulthood, the real world
Old people	People the speaker grew up around	Wisdom and insight into adulthood
Summer	One of the four seasons	Freedom, carefree childhood

Directions: Use the space below to explain what you think the poem "The Rose Bush" means. Use textual evidence and the notes above about the symbolism in the poem to support your answer.

I think that this poem is talking about changing, growing up, and that you can't turn back. I thought that because it says "i don't fit / beneath the rose bushes / anymore" like I couldn't fit into all my old clothes. It says "by my grandmother's porch" which represents that instead of being grandmother's little girl, you're growing up. When it says "the back of the couch / doesn't hide me," I think it means that you can't rely on your parents to get you out of trouble with friends and other people. The lightning could be zits or hormones and things like that, that would unexpectedly strike you, and the "lightning" gets everybody. (Rachel)

Figure 1.3. Student answers (some answers will vary from the ones given above).

Look Down
Jake

little shoes   don't fit
i don't wet the bed
my mom thinks i'm getting tall
school is harder
and knowledge is getting big
learn to read
stay up late

get friends and enemies
start making money
get a girlfriend
get a brother
get homework
i look down and see a child
i look down and see myself yesterday

Learning by Doing

I was in an undergraduate class at Colorado State University the first time I remember being asked to write a variation poem. At first I thought it was a horrible idea. Why should I write a variation of someone else's poem? I knew how to write. Isn't one of the great things about being a poet the ability to say something new or to say something old in a new way? Using someone else's form or subject or words went against everything I believed about the uniqueness of poetry, but I did it anyway because it was an assignment. What happened next was completely unexpected: I loved the poem I wrote. Not only did I love it, but I felt like it was completely mine. The poem I had used as a model, "Poem to be Read at 3:00 A.M." by Donald Justice, was just that, a model. It didn't write my poem for me. I didn't even feel confined by the fact that I was using someone else's idea.

What Would Happen?
Jaime R. Wood

Except for the light
on the stove,
the apartment is dark
at 3 A.M.
with everyone sleeping
but me
and the cat
who seems to always know
when I'm awake
and in need of company.

> Out on the street
> people are talking
> in their middle-of-the-night voices
> not knowing that
> I am awake and
> crying and
> thinking about what would happen
> if I took the roads I was meant to take
> instead of giving up in this apartment
> at 3 A.M.

I took the ideas of light and being one of the only people awake at 3:00 A.M. and used them in my own context. Having a model made the poem faster and less intimidating to write, even for me, a person who enjoys writing poetry.

This section takes three of Nikki Giovanni's poems and explains how they can be used as models for middle school students as they write their own poetry. This creates an opportunity to discuss poetic structure such as line breaks, stanza breaks, spacing, punctuation, capitalization, and any other detail that may add to the meaning of a poem.

Poetic Structure: Line Breaks

"Knoxville, Tennessee" is an effective poem to start with because the language is so easy to understand, and most students can relate to the subject of the warm memories of summer. After reading the poem aloud, ask students to brainstorm a list of things they like best. My students brainstormed things like ice cream, sports, music, animals…the list goes on. Have them choose one of the topics from their lists and write poems using the form of "Knoxville, Tennessee."

While reading the poem aloud, students should focus on specific aspects of the poem. My students focused on Giovanni's use of line breaks and the type of language she used to describe summer.

Knoxville, Tennessee

> I always like summer
> best
> you can eat fresh corn
> from daddy's garden
> and okra
> and greens
> and cabbage
> and lots of
> barbeque
> and buttermilk
> and homemade ice-cream

at the church picnic
and listen to
gospel music
outside
at the church
homecoming
and go to the mountains with
your grandmother
and go barefooted
and be warm
all the time
not only when you go to bed
and sleep

Classroom Snapshot: I was pleasantly surprised when I discussed line breaks and descriptive language with my students because they already had a good idea of why poets might make certain decisions in order to strengthen their poetry. Below I've listed some of the answers I received when I asked about the poem "Knoxville, Tennessee":
What is the purpose of using line breaks?

- Line breaks emphasize certain ideas like when [Giovanni] gives "best" its own line she wants to emphasize that summer really is her favorite. (Eric)
- Line breaks make your brain stop and think for a second longer before you go to the next line. (Mary)

What does Nikki Giovanni do with language to describe summer? Give an example.

- Sensory detail, where they use certain kinds of words that'll spark memories or something and make you imagine it. One example is when she says, "you can eat fresh corn / from daddy's garden." (Jazlyn)

Once I knew that my students had a good grasp of the poem, I asked them to use it as a model for their own poems. I didn't want to give them too many guidelines, but I felt that they needed a few rules to start them off so the assignment would not feel too daunting. I asked them to make their first two lines, "I always like (blank) / best." I also wanted them to keep their poem the same approximate length as Giovanni's, paying close attention to line breaks and sensory images.

Horses
Jazlyn

I always like horses
best
the way their hooves fall
like ballet dancers
step to a tempo
tip tip tap tap
the way they jump
out of the starting
gate
hooves flying
out in time
the sound
of the jockeys
shouting to
their mounts
the way
Hanoverians
glide to the music
horse and
rider
all
one together
at
peace

Classroom Workshop: Revising Word Choice and Order

"Knoxville, Tennessee" can also be used to write a class poem. Class poems are writing exercises that get students to write and revise without becoming so invested in their work that they are not willing to listen to constructive criticism. For students who are not used to receiving critical feedback on their writing, this is an effective way to introduce them to writing workshops. Class poems also give students a way to share language and structure ideas with each other that they can later use in their individual writing.

Choose a subject to fill in the line, "We always like (blank) / best," and ask each student to write a line describing why he or she likes that thing. When putting all the lines together, experiment with arranging the lines in several different ways to show students that poetry allows writers to try multiple ways of looking at lines and words in order to create the meaning that was intended. You can also make copies of all of the lines, put students into groups of three or four, and have each group arrange the lines to their liking. This allows the class to see how the lines can be used in at least four different ways.

Classroom Snapshot: Once my students were put into groups, I gave each group a pair of scissors and a copy of this list. They cut the lines into strips and experimented with the order. I had to remind students again and again that their poems would not be perfect as they were deciding the order of the lines. Revision is a process that should happen more than once, with students focusing on a different skill each time. After students arranged their lines, I put the list of lines on an overhead, and we talked about word choice. We especially focused on vague words or words that were repeated often. Then students returned to their groups and decided on their own word choice changes. During the last revision, every student received a copy of their group's poem, and each student focused on line breaks and any final word choice or line order changes individually. By the end, each student had a poem that looked and sounded fairly different from everyone else's.

Parts of Speech: Verbs

When working with the next poem, "For Tommy," it is important to point out that Giovanni is creating an image of her son through her use of strong verbs. Start by looking at the poem on an overhead and identifying all the verbs in the poem. Before students write their own poems, talk about where the verbs are placed and how they create an image of what kind of child Tommy is. Notice that nearly every line begins with a verb followed by a description. This seems appropriate since Giovanni is writing about an active little boy.

For Tommy

to tommy who:
eats chocolate cookies and lamb chops
climbs stairs and cries when i change
      his diaper
lets me hold him only on his schedule
defined my nature
and gave me a new name (mommy)
which supersedes all others
controls my life
and makes me glad
that he does

Middle school students love to write notes to each other, so this poem is a great way to get them to write a note/poem to someone. Using a skill that students already have (note writing) is an effective way to help them relate to the poetic form, which may be less familiar.

Ask students to think of someone who is really special to them. It can be a family member, a friend, a pet, or someone they "like." With that person in mind, ask students to describe them the way Giovanni describes her son.

Classroom Snapshot: I gave my students only two rules for this poem. The first line of their poems had to be "to (person) who:" and they had to try to use verbs in ways similar to Nikki Giovanni's.

Helen Keller
Amelia

to Helen Keller who:
was blind but she could see
was deaf but she could hear
        different things
showed people how to do things
taught other people
kept learning all her life
who taught us
how to change
she showed the world
that she had freedom of sight

The Function of Form

Middle school is a time of constant change and growth for budding adolescents who are trying to figure out who they are, where they fit in, and what it means not to be a child anymore. That is why friendship is so important during the middle years. Adolescents need to know that they have a place where they belong among their peers. "A Poem of Friendship" talks about the special bond that friends share with each other.

As you read "A Poem of Friendship" with students, talk about the way the stanzas are organized. The poem consists of four stanzas. The first two stanzas have five lines and the second two have four lines. The first two stanzas have the same number of words in each line. The last two stanzas move away from this pattern but still have four lines each. Besides repeating a similar form in each stanza, this poem also repeats a pattern of contrasting descriptions. Studying the form closely will help students think about ways to organize their own writing.

A Poem of Friendship

We are not lovers
because of the love
we make
but the love
we have

We are not friends
because of the laughs
we spend
but the tears
we save

I don't want to be near you
for the thoughts we share
but the words we never have
to speak

I will never miss you
because of what we do
but what we are
together

Animals
Alisson

Animals are
who we want to be
Animals show
what we try to be,
Innocent

Animals try
Animals consider
you their friend
no matter what you look like
no matter if you're cool or not

Animals know
no hate
but fear and
instincts instead

Try to be more
like animals
who do not know
but understand

Extensions

Poetry Workshops

The poetry workshop is a place where students can receive constructive feedback on their writing from their peers before they revise. Generally students work in pairs and focus on specific concepts during each workshop such as word choice (Does the poem include words that are vague or that are not what the author means to say?), readability (Does it make sense?), or form (Could line breaks be used more effectively?), etc. The number and duration of workshops that are held for any given assignment will change according to the number of concepts students work on and the length of the writing assignment.

The idea of a workshop is terrifying for many students because they have to take the risk of being judged by their peers. This is why it is so important for teachers to create a nonthreatening environment when they expect students to give and receive feedback about their writing. The first way to build a safe, positive workshop community is to show students that, by giving "I heard . . ." comments, feedback doesn't have to be positive or negative. Ask for volunteers to read their poems, and explain to the rest of the class that their job is to listen carefully and report back what they remember from the poems. This will show the author that the audience was listening and that there were many memorable moments in their writing.

Once students are ready for suggestions that will help to improve their poetry, it is okay to give both positive and negative feedback. The trick is in the wording. I use the following phrases to take the place of using the words *positive* and *negative feedback*: *stars* and *wishes*, *warm* and *cool feedback*, and *strengths* and *suggestions*. Another way to get students in the workshop mode is to have them make "I notice . . . I wonder . . . If this piece were mine, I would . . ." statements. The order of this workshop practice is important because it moves from safe, positive comments to more critical suggestions. Ask volunteers to share their poems, and ask the class to start by sharing what they notice (these statements should either be positive or neutral) and then what they wonder about the poem (these should be clarifying questions). The last part of this exercise is to have students give suggestions based on what they would add or change if the poem were theirs.

Publishing Student Work

When students have worked to create something of their own, it is essential to find a way to publish because it gives their writing an audience and a purpose. It is one thing for students to write a few poems in class because teachers ask them to, but when they know outside eyes and ears will read or hear their work, they have a whole new reason to be motivated and invested in what they write.

Publishing might mean asking students to choose their favorite poems to frame and put on display in your school. Another option is to create a class anthology after completing several individual and class poems. Students may want to illustrate some of their poems or write author's biographies for the anthology. If your school has a literary journal, encourage students to submit their poetry for publication there. In my community, there are several coffee shops that welcome various types of performance. With your students, organize a poetry reading and invite other students, teachers, and parents to come. Students can create posters and flyers for the event, giving them yet another genre of writing to explore.

2 Li-Young Lee

was introduced to Li-Young Lee's poetry in 2003 at a Writing Project Summer Institute held at Colorado State University. It was thrilling to spend four weeks with a group of teachers who were passionate about literature and writing, so thrilling that we couldn't seem to get enough of the experience. Several of us decided to meet once a week during lunch to share poetry that had been an inspiration in our lives. We read our favorite poems by Naomi Shihab Nye, Sharon Olds, Nikki Giovanni, and performance poet Taylor Mali, but I will never forget the day my friend Cameron brought in his favorite Li-Young Lee poem and read it to us.

Persimmons

In sixth grade Mrs. Walker
slapped the back of my head
and made me stand in the corner
for not knowing the difference
between *persimmon* and *precision*.
How to choose

persimmons. This is precision.
Ripe ones are soft and brown-spotted.
Sniff the bottoms. The sweet one
will be fragrant. How to eat:
put the knife away, lay down newspaper.
Peel the skin tenderly, not to tear the meat.
Chew the skin, suck it,
and swallow. Now, eat
the meat of the fruit,
so sweet,
all of it, to the heart.

Donna undresses, her stomach is white.
In the yard, dewy and shivering
with crickets, we lie naked,
face-up, face down.
I teach her Chinese.
Crickets: *chui chui*. Dew: I've forgotten.
Naked: I've forgotten.
Ni, wo: you and me.
I part her legs,
remember to tell her
she is beautiful as the moon.

Other words
that got me into trouble were
fight and *fright*, *wren* and *yarn*.
Fight was what I did when I was frightened,
fright was what I felt when I was fighting.
Wrens are small, plain birds,
yarn is what one knits with.
Wrens are soft as yarn.
My mother made birds out of yarn.
I loved to watch her tie the stuff;
a bird, a rabbit, a wee man.

Mrs. Walker brought a persimmon to class
and cut it up
so everyone could taste
a *Chinese apple*. Knowing
it wasn't ripe or sweet, I didn't eat
but watched the other faces.

My mother said every persimmon has a sun
inside, something golden, glowing,
warm as my face.

Once, in the cellar, I found two wrapped in newspaper,
forgotten and not yet ripe.
I took them and set both on my bedroom windowsill,
where each morning a cardinal
sang, *The sun, the sun.*

Finally understanding
he was going blind,
my father sat up all one night
waiting for a song, a ghost.
I gave him the persimmons,
swelled, heavy as sadness,
and sweet as love.

This year, in the muddy lighting
of my parents' cellar, I rummage, looking
for something I lost.
My father sits on the tired, wooden stairs,
black cane between his knees,
hand over hand, gripping the handle.

He's so happy that I've come home.
I ask how his eyes are, a stupid question.
All gone, he answers.

Under some blankets, I find a box.
Inside the box I find three scrolls.
I sit beside him and untie
three paintings by my father:
Hibiscus leaf and a white flower.

Two cats preening.
Two persimmons, so full they want to drop from the cloth.

He raises both hands to touch the cloth,
asks, *Which is this?*

This is persimmons, Father.

Oh, the feel of the wolftail on the silk,
the strength, the tense,
precision in the wrist.
I painted them hundreds of times
eyes closed. These I painted blind.
Some things never leave a person:
scent of the hair of one you love,
the texture of persimmons,
in your palm, the ripe weight.

I was speechless, astonished by the images, the language, and the way Li-Young Lee played with line breaks and rhyme in a seamless way. I couldn't figure him out. How did he do it? How did he manage to leave me wanting to know what persimmons taste like, feeling as though I needed to save him from Mrs. Walker who could not possibly understand what true precision of language is, and desperately wanting to see the paintings that his father could not? The only explanation is that Lee is a magician. He gives his audience an art that fills them with wonder and excitement, but never reveals his craft.

In this chapter, Lee's poetry will take students on a language journey. They will explore images and stories that they will not soon forget. The goal is to examine these poems in such a way that students will see the magic and begin to understand the craft of poetry.

Precision: Language as a Tool

How many times have you read a story or a paper written by one of your students that uses the same language again and again? Not only is it repetitive, it's vague, and quite frankly, it's boring:

- The girl is nice.
- Things are happening.
- The stuff is cool.
- That day was good.
- This is big.

These sentences leave the reader with nothing but questions. Who is the girl? What makes her nice? What exactly is happening? When? Where? Should I be happy about these things happening, or should I panic? You get the picture. The bad news is that this isn't even the worst of it. Middle school students have a hard time saying what they mean and meaning what they say. Poetry can really help with this problem of language precision. Students will use the poem in this section to examine the image-invoking language in Li-Young Lee's poetry and to compare it to the ordinary language they are accustomed to writing.

Prereading: Solving a Riddle

Before putting students into groups of three or four, explain that each group will receive one or two words, depending on how many groups there are. The words they will work with are *rice, boiling, fire, morning, combs* (verb form), *thick, sound, fifty,* and *hair.* (It is important that each group only sees their own words.) Also, explain that each group should have a recorder, a dictionary/thesaurus searcher, and a presenter. The recorder will list the members of the group and their roles on the same piece of paper where notes are to be taken. Groups will describe their word(s) as vividly as they possibly can without using the word in their description. They can use a dictionary and a thesaurus since understanding the definitions, synonyms, and antonyms for the words may help students gain a better idea of how to describe them. Remind students that the goal of describing something is to create a clear image in the minds of the people who read or hear the description.

Some classes may need to see an example before they get started. Choose one of the words from the list or think of another word that is reasonably concrete, brainstorm ways to describe the word with the whole class, and write ideas on the board. It may also be a good idea to model how to use the dictionary and thesaurus for this exercise.

After groups have described their words, each presenter should read to the rest of the class what their group created. Give the other groups three tries to guess what is being described. If students have not guessed the word after three tries, the presenter can tell them the answer. This is a good opportunity for students to give constructive feedback. If the word was easily guessed from the description, give students a chance to explain what parts of the description gave it away. If the word was not guessed, students can give examples of other ways in which the word could have been described more effectively.

Reading

After all groups have read their descriptions, write the nine words on the board and explain that the class is going to read a poem that uses descriptions or synonyms of these words. (You might want to mix the word list up a bit because I listed the words in the order that the descriptions/synonyms appear in the poem.) Give the students a copy of "Early in the Morning" and the T-chart in Figure 2.1. Read the poem twice. Students should read along the first time. During the second reading, they should look for the descriptions or synonyms of the words and record them on the right side of the T-chart. After giving students a few minutes to complete their charts, have the class share their answers.

Early in the Morning

While the long grain is softening
in the water, gurgling
over a low stove flame, before
the salted Winter Vegetable is sliced
for breakfast, before the birds,
my mother glides an ivory comb
through her hair, heavy
and black as calligrapher's ink.

She sits at the foot of the bed.
My father watches, listens for
the music of the comb
against hair.

My mother combs,
pulls her hair back
tight, rolls it
around two fingers, pins it
in a bun to the back of her head.
For half a hundred years she has done this.
My father likes to see it like this.
He says it is kempt.

But I know
it is because of the way
my mother's hair falls
when he pulls the pins out.
Easily, like the curtains
when they untie them in the evening.

Discussion: Turning on the Light

A detailed study of the language in poetry can be like turning on the comprehension light for students. It allows them to look closely at each word and make decisions about what the words mean and ultimately how they function as part of the poem. After doing an exercise like the one above, it is important to take it a step further by discussing the ways in which the language in the poem can lead to a better understanding of the poem's content.

Language Match
Directions: Match the word in the left column with the description or synonym from the poem. Write the description/synonym in the right column.

Word	Description/Synonym
rice	"long grain"
boiling	"gurgling"
fire	"a low stove flame"
morning	"before/ the salted Winter Vegetable is sliced/ for breakfast, before the birds,"
combs (verb form)	"glides"
thick	"heavy/ and black as calligrapher's ink."
sound	"the music of comb"
fifty	"half a hundred years"
hair	"like the curtains/ when they untie them in the evening."

Figure 2.1. Answer key.

Talk as a class about how the use of vivid language changes the meaning and the tone of the poem. Below are some possible questions to spark discussion about "Early in the Morning." When asking these questions, keep in mind that it is okay and even good for students to have multiple readings of a poem as long as they can support their readings with examples from the poem.

You may also want to turn this into a think-pair-share activity. Start by giving each student a number. Students will work individually to answer the questions that correspond with their numbers. They will then meet with other students who share their number to compare answers. Give each group a few minutes to choose a reporter and come to consensus about the answers they will report to the rest of the class. The reporters can then either tell the class the answers to their questions or they can write the answers on the board or on a piece of butcher paper to display on the wall.

1. Substitute the descriptions or synonyms in the poem with the words from the list. Compare this poem to Lee's original poem. How do the words from the list affect the way the poem sounds and feels?

2. Why do you think Lee uses the words and phrases that he does?

3. What are some things that happen early in the morning in this poem?

4. Based on the description of the mother, what do you think she looks like? (Some students may want to draw a picture of her.)

5. What do you think Lee is saying about his parents? What kind of relationship do you think they have?

6. What do you think this poem is about? What from the poem makes you think that?

Extensions

Transference

Now that students have a basic understanding of what precise language is and why writers use it, it is time to see if they can transfer this new knowledge to other areas. Take a paragraph or a story from a literature book and prepare the paragraph or story ahead of time by taking out all of the descriptive language for the students. Give the students the "boring copy" and ask them to revise it to include more vibrant language. Again, they may want to use the dictionary or thesaurus for this activity.

Paint a Scene

Ask students to choose a time of day, such as early in the morning or late at night, and ask them to freewrite about their chosen time. Once they finish freewriting, ask them to trade their papers with a partner of their choice. Partners should look for words that could be more descriptive and circle them. Students can then revise the work on their own or collaborate with their partners to find better ways of using language. It is helpful to have someone else look at students' work because they are sometimes so close to their own writing that they cannot accurately see what needs to be revised.

Using Metaphors to Create Meaning

Most middle school students are not aware of it, but they use metaphors all the time. Anytime students compare two things that are not really all that alike, they are using metaphors. How many students do you know who collect CDs, posters, stickers, or stuffed animals? How many of them can tell you the meaning behind each of their favorite collectables? This is the beginning of metaphorical thinking.

Making It Personal: Bio Bags

Before students try to identify metaphors in poetry, they should name some important metaphors from their own lives. One entertaining way to do this is to have students create *bio bags*. A bio bag is a collection of things that students bring in from home that are important to them. When I do this, students bring in a wide variety of objects from pictures to toys to their favorite songs. I usually give students a specific number of things to bring, and I start by sharing my own bio bag with them. Mine consists of a picture of my family, some of my poetry, my college diploma, a souvenir from Europe, and one of my cat's toys. On the day students bring their bio bags in, we sit in a circle, usually on the floor, and share. The prompt is, "What is in your bag and why are these objects important to you?" Each student should get at least five minutes to share. Even though this may take a full class period to complete, it's worth taking the time to hear students' voices and to learn something about them you may not have known before.

After sharing bio bags, the next step is for students to decide what their objects are metaphorically. Talk about the fact that each of the objects has a literal and a figurative meaning. For example, my diploma is literally a piece of paper with some words on it, but metaphorically it is a journey, a wealth of knowledge, and a ticket to the career I want. Explain to students that a metaphor, like a simile, is a comparison of two things, but the difference is that metaphors do not use *like* or *as*. Have students use the web in Figure 2.2 to make a list of everything in their bags and to write metaphors for each object. I have included my own bio web in Figure 2.2 as an example.

Classroom Snapshot: I have to admit that I expected my students to catch on to writing metaphors quickly and easily, and when they didn't I had to reevaluate what a metaphor is and why they were getting confused. When my class completed their bio webs, many stu-

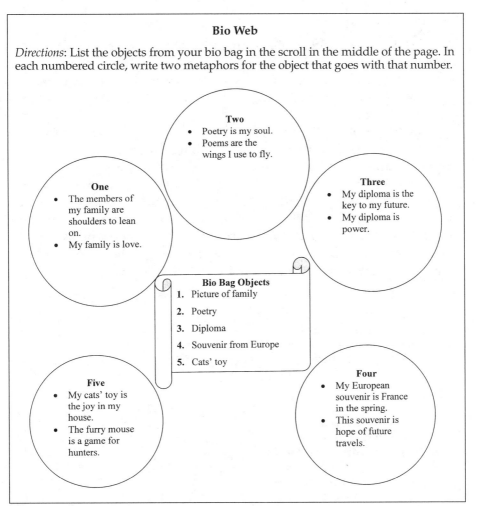

Figure 2.2. Teacher's example.

dents wrote things like "My video game is fun," thinking that this was a metaphor. To help them get a better grasp on metaphors, I required that they take two concrete objects or nouns and compare them to each other. For example, one student brought in his favorite book, *Call of the Wild*, and compared it to a storm. When I asked him to explain his metaphor, he said that like a storm, *Call of the Wild* is unpredictable and the reader can get carried away in it. Once students understood that metaphors are not just descriptions of nouns using adjectives, they were much more successful at writing metaphors using the objects in their bio bags.

Reading and Discussion

In "The Gift," Lee writes about a memory of his father pulling a splinter from his hand and what that moment means to him. Lee uses metaphors to convey powerful imagery and emotion in this poem, just as students used metaphors to explain what is important about the objects in their bio bags.

Read the poem aloud once so that students can become familiar with it. After the first reading, ask students to share their initial responses to this poem. Once students have had a chance to discuss it, read the poem a second time asking students to underline all of the objects that are being compared to each other. Now students are ready to share some of the words or phrases they identified in the poem before moving on. Record these possible metaphors on the board for students to reference as they work. It may be necessary to use one of these as an example to explain the following activity.

The Gift

To pull the splinter from my palm
my father recited a story in a low voice.
I watched his lovely face and not the blade.
Before the story ended, he'd removed
the iron sliver I thought I'd die from.

I can't remember the tale,
but hear his voice still, a well
of dark water, a prayer.
And I recall his hands,
two measures of tenderness
he laid against my face,
the flames of discipline
he raised above my head.

Had you entered that afternoon
you would have thought you saw a man
planting something in a boy's palm,
a silver tear, a tiny flame.
Had you followed that boy
you would have arrived here,
where I bend over my wife's right hand.

Look how I shave her thumbnail down
so carefully she feels no pain.
Watch as I lift the splinter out.
I was seven when my father
took my hand like this,

and I did not hold that shard
between my fingers and think,
Metal that will bury me,
christen it Little Assassin,
Ore Going Deep for My Heart.
And I did not lift up my wound and cry,
Death visited here!
I did what a child does
when he's given something to keep.
I kissed my father.

Activity

Give students the graphic organizer in Figure 2.3 and ask them to work
individually to identify the metaphors in the poem and explain what
each metaphor means. Once students have finished the chart portion
of the sheet, they should work to answer the synthesizing questions on
the second half of the sheet. Explain that these questions should be answered in full sentences and should include examples from the poem
to support students' answers. They may want to check their answers
with a partner before sharing with the class.

Extensions

The Metaphor Challenge

Find objects that can be paired together to create metaphors. For example, a piece of paper might be paired with a feather, or a leaf with a
grocery bag. Put students into groups of three or four and give each
group a pair of objects. Their challenge is to do two things: write two
metaphors such as "the paper is a feather" and "the feather is paper"
and explain how these two objects work together to make a metaphor.
Give volunteers a chance to share their metaphors and explanations with
the rest of the class. This is a concrete way to help students grasp metaphorical thinking and can also work as a writing prompt. Once the class
has completed this activity, students can use their metaphors as a line
in a poem or story.

Father: Visualizing the Character

Although poetry is not usually the genre used to teach students about
characterization, Li-Young Lee writes about people, mainly his family,
quite a bit in his poetry. He describes his relationship to his wife, mother,
and father, and he creates vivid pictures of these people and what they

Metaphorical Meaning

Directions: List all of the objects from the poem in the left column, what the object was compared with in the middle column, and a brief explanation for each answer in the right column. The explanation column might include information about why the metaphor means what it does or it might describe how the metaphor helps the reader understand the meaning of the poem. *You may need more space to write the explanations. Use the back of this sheet or a separate piece of paper if necessary.

Object	Metaphor	Explanation
splinter	"a silver tear, a tiny flame." "*Metal that will bury me,*" "Little Assassin" "Ore Going Deep for My Heart."	The splinter is a sharp pain, hence "flame," and I also think a tear is similar to the size of a splinter. (Forrest) He was just a little boy so he turned this little thing into an assassin that was "going deep for my heart," when all it was, was a small splinter. (Keller)
his voice (the father's)	"…a well / of dark water, a prayer."	The voice is calm and quiet like a dark well. The boy probably doesn't know what is coming next. It's comforting and sounds safe to the boy. (Lynn) Safety like a prayer gives you a sense of security knowing someone's there. (Paige)
his hands (the father's)	"two measures of tenderness /he laid against my face, / the flames of discipline / he raised above my head."	It explains how tender he could be and how just a gentle touch can make you feel better and not as afraid. The discipline is for the splinter. (Mary) His hands, although gentle and soft, showed discipline of the task at hand. (Tommy)

Synthesizing Meaning

Directions: Read the following questions carefully and use the space below to record your answers. Please answer the questions in complete sentences and include examples from the poem to support your answers.
- Why do you think this memory was important enough for Lee to write a poem about?
- What might this memory represent?
- What from the poem makes you believe this?
- Why is the poem called "The Gift"?

continued on next page

Figure 2.3. Student answers (some correct explanations may vary from the ones shown above).

Figure 2.3 continued

> I think this memory was important enough for Lee to write about because the story and its lesson still held in his mind after all these years. I think this because the poem says "I…hear his voice still…," and although not directly, he soothed his wife the same way his father soothed him. I think this memory might represent Lee's love for his father. I think this because throughout the poem it kept referring to him and his father, and at the end it said he "…did what a child does / when he's given something to keep. / [he] kissed [his] father." (Keller)
>
> I think this memory was important enough to write about because he learned from it. Later he used the knowledge on his wife and helped her take a splinter out. "Had you followed that boy / you would have arrived here, / where I bend over my wife's right hand." I also think it was a comforting memory Lee wanted to share. It represents his father and how he is kind in his actions. "I watched his lovely face and not the blade." The description and detail of the poem made me believe it. "Before the story ended, he'd removed / the iron sliver I thought I'd die from." (Lynn)

mean to him. The three poems in this lesson are all about Lee's father, and they are used to teach students how to create a *body biography* of a character. This idea was adapted from a lesson originally shared by William Underwood in his *English Journal* article "The Body Biography: A Framework for Student Writing," where he had students create body autobiographies to teach them about metaphor and themselves.

Prereading: You're a Character

Breaking a person or character into categories allows students to focus on specific aspects of who they are instead of just describing themselves in a general way. In order to help students better understand how to describe a character, give them the "You're a Character" organizer shown in Figure 2.4, and ask them to work in pairs to characterize their partners using these four categories: personality, physical attributes, emotions, and thoughts.

   After students have made lists describing their partners, they should exchange papers, choose one characteristic from each category, and draw a picture of that characteristic in each box of the "You're a Character" sheet. Lastly, students will label their pictures to explain where on their bodies the images best fit.

Figure 2.4. Student example.

Classroom Snapshot: This activity proved to be especially difficult for students when they were asked to move away from drawing smiley faces or stick figures. I wanted them to be able to describe themselves metaphorically by using objects that they might not typically associate with themselves, like the rose that one student drew to represent her rosy cheeks. Once they got the hang of it, students came up with new, creative images to describe their partners. One of my students described himself as "tall" in the physical category, drew a big pine tree, and said that he would put the tree on his legs. Another student described herself as "excited" in the emotional category. She drew a lightning bolt and wanted to place it in her heart.

Reading

Because this lesson uses three poems, it is helpful to read all three of them with students before asking the class to focus on individual poems in groups. After reading the poems aloud, spend a few minutes asking questions so students can explain briefly what they thought each poem was about, but do not spend too much time on this part since students will have ample chance to synthesize the meanings of the poems later.

"Words for Worry" is a good poem to start with because it is reasonably easy to understand, and it lists several things the father does and shows how the father feels about the child in the poem. Another reason it makes sense to read this poem first is because it shows the father in the state of fatherhood, whereas the next two poems are reflections about the father after he is gone.

Words for Worry

Another word for *father* is *worry.*

Worry boils the water
for tea in the middle of the night.

Worry trimmed the child's nails before
singing him to sleep.

Another word for *son* is *delight*,
another word, *hidden.*

And another is *One-Who-Goes-Away.*
Yet another, *One-Who-Returns.*

So many words for son:
He-Dreams-for-All-Our-Sakes.
His-Play-Vouchsafes-Our-Winter-Share.
His-Dispersal-Wins-the-Birds.

But only one word for *father*.
And sometimes a man is both.
Which is to say sometimes a man
manifests mysteries beyond
his own understanding.

For instance, being the one and the many,
and the loneliness of either. Or

the living light we see by, we never see. Or

the sole word weighs
heavy as a various name.

And sleepless worry folds the laundry for tomorrow.
Tired worry wakes the child for school.

Orphan worry writes the note he hides
in the child's lunch bag.
It begins, *Dear Firefly. . . .*

In "Mnemonic" the speaker is reflecting on his father after he passed away. This poem serves as a sort of mnemonic device for the speaker to remember his father, and it gives a brief description of the father's personality in the third stanza ("A serious man who devised complex systems of numbers and / rhymes / to aid him in remembering, a man who forgot nothing, my father / would be ashamed of me"), which will help students get to know him a little better.

Mnemonic

I was tired. So I lay down.
My lids grew heavy. So I slept.
Slender memory, stay with me.

I was cold once. So my father took off his blue sweater.
He wrapped me in it, and I never gave it back.
It is the sweater he wore to America,
this one, which I've grown into, whose sleeves are too long,
whose elbows have thinned, who outlives its rightful owner.
Flamboyant blue in daylight, poor blue by daylight,
it is black in the folds.

A serious man who devised complex systems of numbers and
    rhymes
to aid him in remembering, a man who forgot nothing, my
    father
would be ashamed of me.
Not because I'm forgetful,
but because there is no order
to my memory, a heap
of details, uncatalogued, illogical.
For instance:

God was lonely. So he made me.
My father loved me. So he spanked me.
It hurt him to do so. He did it daily.

The earth is flat. Those who fall off don't return.
The earth is round. All things reveal themselves to men only
    gradually.

I won't last. Memory is sweet.
Even when it's painful, memory is sweet.

Once I was cold. So my father took off his blue sweater.

The last poem in this section, "Eating Together," describes a lunch that the speaker eats with his family. As his mother tastes the fish, the speaker remembers his father, who is now gone. While the father is only mentioned briefly in this poem, much can be learned from asking questions about the scene in this poem.

Eating Together

In the steamer is the trout
seasoned with slivers of ginger,
two sprigs of green onion, and sesame oil.
We shall eat it with rice for lunch,
brothers, sister, my mother who will
taste the sweetest meat of the head,
holding it between her fingers
deftly, the way my father did
weeks ago. Then he lay down
to sleep like a snow-covered road
winding through pines older than him,
without any travelers, and lonely for no one.

Cooperative Learning: Extracting the Character

Once students have a basic grasp of the three poems, they are ready to set out in groups to study one poem thoroughly. The steps to this group activity are listed below.

- Every student will need a character card like the ones shown in Figure 2.5.
- Each group will have a student with a personality card, a physical card, an emotion card, and a thought card, making groups of four. If for some reason there is a group of three, the whole group can be responsible for the fourth character card.
- Give each group one poem to work on. (Depending on your class size, there will be two or three groups working on the same poem. That's okay. When it comes time to share, ask the groups to share only things that have not already been said by another group.)

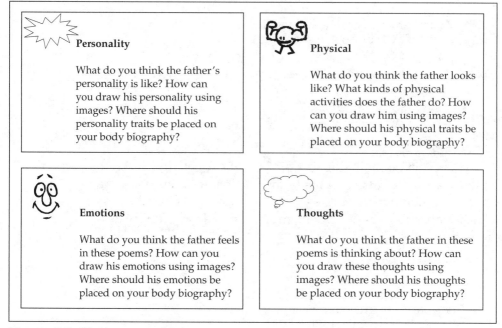

Figure 2.5. Character cards.

- Students will answer the questions on their character cards by underlining sections of their poems and drawing images in the margins of their poems. Remind them that they should label where they want to place the images on their body biographies.

While students are still in groups, ask them to share what they have discovered about the father in their poems. Give each group a chance to question other groups, especially those who studied a different poem. Make sure students understand that they will be responsible for understanding all three poems as they work on their body biographies, so they should take notes and underline important passages as different groups share.

Each poem reveals different aspects of the father. For example, in the poem "Words for Worry," the father does several things such as boil water, trim the son's nails, and fold laundry that show a good deal about him. Besides explaining the types of physical activities that this father participates in, this poem also shows how the father feels about the son based on what he does for him.

In "Mnemonic," readers learn that the father is a serious man who uses mnemonic devices "to aid him in remembering" (*Rose* 13). They also learn that the father is strict with his son: "My father loved me. So he spanked me" (21). This gives insight into what the father thinks about as well as his personality. Once again, the father is compassionate toward his son in this poem. "I was cold once. So my father took off his blue sweater. / He wrapped me in it, and I never gave it back" (4–5).

The most challenging poem in this lesson is probably "Eating Together" because it is a scene without the father, but students can still learn quite a bit about the father here. This is the only poem that shows what and how the father ate before he passed away: "my mother who will / taste the sweetest meat of the head, / holding it between her fingers / deftly, the way my father did / weeks ago" (*Rose* 5–9). The most telling lines appear at the end of the poem when readers learn that the father is gone and that he seems to be peaceful in death. "Then he lay down / to sleep like a snow-covered road / winding through pines older than him, / without any travelers, and lonely for no one" (9–12).

This should provide enough information about the father for students to start creating images based on what they learn through these poems. Remind students that the images should represent the characteristics they are describing. For instance, placing a calculator in the father's brain might be a good way to show that he used numbers as a mnemonic device.

Activity: The Body Biography

The purpose of the body biography is for students to show that they understand the father well enough to make a representation of him using images and passages from the poems, paying attention to where things are placed on the body. Students should stay in their groups for this activity so that they can continue to use their character cards to delegate responsibilities. If a student has a personality card, for example, he or she will be responsible for choosing lines from each poem and corresponding images that describe the father's personality. Each group should have the following materials to complete the body biographies:

- all three poems,
- butcher paper to trace the body,
- colored pencils or markers,
- construction paper, and
- tape or glue.

Figure 2.6. Student example.

Classroom Snapshot: I asked my students to include one image and quote for each aspect of the father—physical, personality, emotion, thought—because I wanted to emphasize the importance of choosing images that make sense with the quotes from the poems (see Figure 2.6). Some of my students focused more on one or two poems instead of pulling information from all three. If I had had more time, I would have required that each body biography include more images and quotes and that they use all three poems.

Extension

Reflection

Sometimes project-based assignments like the body biography are passed up because it is not clear how to assess what students have learned from them. Even when students produce quality work, it is difficult to ascertain how they make decisions such as what images to represent certain characteristics and where to place the images on the body.

This is a perfect opportunity to ask students to reflect on their work. Groups can divide up the images on their body biographies, and each group member can write a reflection. The reflection should answer how they chose their images and why they placed them where they did on the body. In the end, students should be able to explain why a necktie, for example, represents the father's serious nature, and why the necktie might be placed around his head instead of in its usual position.

3 Pat Mora

A good poem gives me chills or brings me to tears or makes me think and question the world or myself. A great poem does all of these things. The first Pat Mora poem I ever read was shared with me by my graduate school advisor. It is this poem that convinced me that I needed to include Pat Mora's work in this book.

Immigrants

wrap their babies in the American flag,
feed them mashed hot dogs and apple pie,
name them Bill and Daisy,
buy them blonde dolls that blink blue
eyes or a football and tiny cleats
before the baby can even walk,
speak to them in thick English,
        hallo, babee, hallo,
whisper in Spanish or Polish
when the babies sleep, whisper
in a dark parent bed, that dark
parent fear, "Will they like
our boy, our girl, our fine american
boy, our fine american girl?"

When I finished reading this poem for the first time, I was simultaneously outraged and inspired. These parents wanted their children to be accepted so badly in America that they worked to hide where they came from and who they were. At the same time, this poem tells the history of our country. This is the story of every immigrant who has ever wanted a different life for his or her family, who has ever dreamed of new possibilities in a new world.

Pat Mora brings readers closer to humanity by writing with such honesty and insight about everything from racial issues to the moon. In this chapter, students will explore poetry through their senses, use personification to describe the inanimate world, and create theme boxes with the help of Pat Mora's nurturing voice.

Sensory Imagery

One of the best ways I've found to get students to write really specific descriptions is to have them use all of their senses to talk about something small, like a grain of rice or a piece of chocolate. I start out using food for this lesson because it lends itself so easily to most of the five senses, but it is also fun to take students outside and imagine what other objects are like. What does a cloud smell like? How does it sound if you're in the middle of it? How would it feel if it brushed across your face? Can you taste it? What different things can a cloud look like in a span of five minutes?

In this lesson, students practice using their senses by describing various objects and writing their own sensory poems before being asked to discuss the sensory images they find in the poem "Echoes." By the end of this lesson, not only should students be able to identify sensory images, but they should also be able to explain how sensory images contribute to a poem's meaning.

Groups: Sharing the Senses

When students go outside to explore such sensory-rich experiences as lying in grass, staring up at clouds, or blowing bubbles, it should be an individual activity. Contemplating the many aspects of the natural world requires a bit of solitude and reflection, after all. But the first time students delve into their senses, give them the organizer shown in Figure 3.1, put them into groups of three or four, and provide the groups with paper bags full of edible mysteries. Encourage students to feel and smell their objects before they look at them. This tends to allow for more imaginative sensory images. Also, remind students that the goal of this activity is not to guess what the objects are, but rather to describe them in detail using all five senses.

Practice: Writing a Sensory Poem

Right after students have finished working in groups to complete the "Using Your Senses" organizer, ask them to share their answers by reading each box without stopping. As the example demonstrates, this activity alone can create poetry, and students will be astounded at what they create without even meaning to. This is a good time to have students write a sensory poem. Ask them to use one of the objects they started with or choose something new to write about. The goal is for them to use their senses to describe something so well that their audience senses it too. The two examples below accomplished this goal.

The Apple Basket
Patricia

Skipping down the green grass meadow
Along the trees that stand like an
Elephant's foot

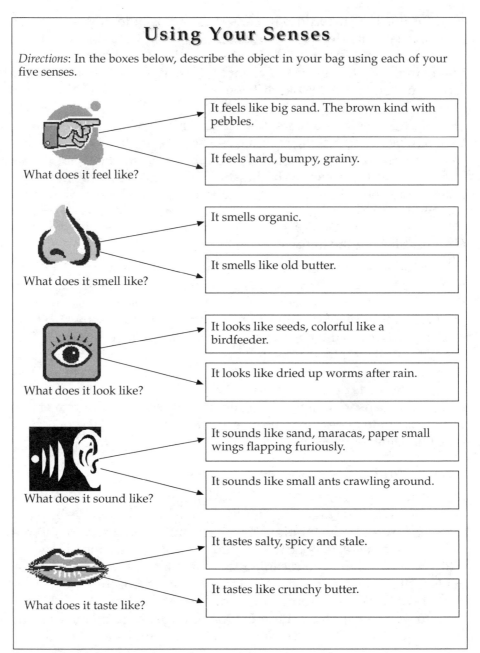

Using Your Senses

Directions: In the boxes below, describe the object in your bag using each of your five senses.

What does it feel like?

It feels like big sand. The brown kind with pebbles.

It feels hard, bumpy, grainy.

What does it smell like?

It smells organic.

It smells like old butter.

What does it look like?

It looks like seeds, colorful like a birdfeeder.

It looks like dried up worms after rain.

What does it sound like?

It sounds like sand, maracas, paper small wings flapping furiously.

It sounds like small ants crawling around.

What does it taste like?

It tastes salty, spicy and stale.

It tastes like crunchy butter.

Figure 3.1. Student answers (the object described above is uncooked wild rice).

Carrying the apple basket with
The wind rustling the leaves

The golden red apples looking extra
Fruity today
It's time to pick the apples
That look juicy in May

Toe Shoes
Daniella

sweet warm blood
softly flowing down toes
which are covered in painful blisters
from a hard hopeful ballet class

the stress of knowing when the day
will come
of silence and brains ticking and judgments
being made
from the slightest movement you make
whether it is a fault or a success
both making the stomach jerk into knots
just trying to make your body do
something or insist on making
it better

but who can fix the fault
of forgetting to cover
the pesky growing blisters
before putting on the
supporting yet punishing
shoes
which leave sweet warm blood
softly flowing down your toes

Reading: Relating the Senses to a Text

Now that students have experience using their senses in several different ways, they are prepared to read "Echoes," a Pat Mora poem that
uses beautiful sensory imagery to tell a story.

Echoes

I sipped white wine
with the women in cool dresses
and sculptured nails shimmering
in the May heat as our children
whacked the piñata whirling
in the desert wind, candy
and colored paper tossed carelessly.

In her white uniform, Magdalena
set the table remembering such laughter
at fiestas in Zacatecas, enjoying
the afternoon's songs and games,
trying to snare English words floating
in the air like the children's
carefree balloons.

Her smile wavered when I spoke
to her in Spanish. Perhaps she wondered
why I'd leave the other señoras,
join her when she served, why I'd
drift to the edge.

Again and again I hear:
    just drop the cups and plates
    on the grass. My maid
    will pick them up.
Again and again I feel
my silence, the party whirring around me.

I longed to hear this earth
roar, to taste thunder,
to see proper smiles twist
as those black words echoed
in the wind again and again:
    just drop . . .
    my maid
    just drop . . .
    my maid

Perhaps my desert land waits
to hear me roar, waits to hear
me flash: NO.   NO.
Again and again.

Classroom Snapshot: I wasn't sure what my students would think of
this poem when I read it to them the first time. I thought they would
be able to identify the sensory images easily enough, but would they
understand what the speaker is going through? Would they sympa-
thize with her? Would they be angry, too? Surprisingly enough, the
answer to all of these questions is yes. As we discussed the poem, I
asked students to tell me how it made them feel, and many of them
said that they wished the speaker had done more to help Magdalena.
They thought the women at the party were selfish and unfair, and
one boy wished Magdalena had just walked out. That opened up the
conversation to talk about immigration and workers' rights in

America and Mexico. I suppose this could be something to be weary of since this sort of discussion tends to steer students miles away from the larger purpose of the lesson, but I value any opportunity to relate literature to current events and cultural issues. I like to think that making these kinds of connections is really the larger purpose for exposing students to poems like "Echoes."

When I decided to use this poem to teach sensory imagery, I was excited about having the opportunity to incorporate a geography minilesson to help students better comprehend the poem. It is important to note that, while there is no way of knowing exactly where this poem takes place, my students were very observant of the fact that it is in a hot desert and probably in America, based on Magdalena's position. Many of my students imagined that Pat Mora, who lives in Santa Fe, New Mexico, was the speaker in this poem. Even if she is not the speaker, several students noted, she seems to be writing from experience. Keeping that in mind, I thought it was important to show students just how close we are to all that is taking place in this poem. I did this by taping a huge map of North America to my white board and asking for three volunteers to come up and act as pins pointing out three locations: Colorado (to locate themselves), New Mexico (to locate Pat Mora), and Zacatecas, Mexico (to find the place mentioned in the poem). Once they had their fingers on the correct places, I asked for two more volunteers to measure the distance between each place, especially the distance between Colorado and the other two places. I also used a map to give a more detailed view of Zacatecas. After passing out the poem, I asked students to locate the word *Zacatecas* in the second stanza, circle it, and write in the margin its distance from Colorado, which we learned was approximately 1,200 miles, closer to my students than the eastern seaboard of the United States.

Writing: Explaining the Images

Read the poem to students twice. During the first reading, they can either read along or underline places where they see Pat Mora using one of the five senses to describe something. By the time the poem has been read twice, students should have labeled which senses are used next to each underlined passage. During classroom discussion, students should be able to explain what the poem is about and how sensory imagery works to make the poem more meaningful or easier to understand. Have each student write a paragraph explaining what "Echoes" is about and how the sensory images affect the poem's meaning. Students should use textual evidence in the form of paraphrased or quoted examples from the poem to support their answers.

"Echoes" Explanation
Paige

Pat Mora's poem, "Echoes," vividly describes the meaning and mood of the poem by using sensory images. At the beginning of the poem it was talking about white wine and cool dresses which give you a feel of upper-class elegance. Yet when it went from the white wine to the white uniform it changed the class of the hostess and the maid. When it mentioned that the maid's smile wavered when the speaker started to talk to her, it showed the level of amazement that the maid felt. However, the end, when it talks about hearing the cruel comment of "just drop the cups and plates / on the grass," it gave the poem a feeling of darkness as the poem told how the speaker stood in silence which describes her contradicting feelings. Towards the end of the poem the roar and flash help the reader envision the speaker's rage for the cruelty that is being calmed in a racist society.

As the above example demonstrates, students are able to interpret this relatively complicated poem by focusing on one literary device. They use the sensory images in "Echoes" as tools to understand larger, more symbolic concepts such as social barriers and class systems.

Extension

Incorporating Creative Techniques into Academic Writing

Students enjoy learning how to write using techniques such as sensory imagery because these techniques provide a whole new way to communicate. They tend to grasp how to use them in creative writing assignments, but the trick is helping students understand how to incorporate these new tools into more structured academic genres such as essays. Since students were briefly introduced to Zacatecas, Mexico, during this lesson, this is a perfect place to start. Assign students to gather five to ten facts about a specific aspect of Zacatecas such as tourism, climate, industry, food, culture, etc. to bring back and share with the rest of the class. Have them post the facts on a piece of butcher paper so that students can easily access them as they write. They can choose one or two related areas to write a one-page report on using sensory images in their writing. Explain that sensory images make everything easier for the mind to visualize, so if a student is writing a paper on the climate in Zacatecas, for instance, the report will be much more powerful if the climate has smell, sound, and color as well as feeling.

Personification

Literary devices are everywhere, and students are practicing them all the time without even knowing it. How many seventh graders have you heard using hyperbole, for example? Personification is another device that kids know before they have a word for it. Clocks have hands and faces. Books have spines. Sunlight dances and the moon soothes us to sleep. We are constantly trying to depict the world in terms we can relate to more easily, and giving human characteristics to nonhuman things is one way to accomplish this goal.

Prereading: Bring It to Life

To introduce personification, start by giving students a model of a riddle to use while they write their own riddles later. Place the riddle in Figure 3.2, or one like it, on an overhead, and read it aloud asking the class to guess what they think the object is.

Once they have guessed that the object in the riddle is a clock, tell them that human characteristics are used to describe the clock, and ask them to identify as many human characteristics as they can find. Discuss with the class the fact that personification makes a nonhuman thing seem more human by adding characteristics such as gender, emotions, human-like actions, and physical traits to the object. Many times students will already know what personification is, but they may never have been asked to use it in their own writing.

Now that they have seen an example of a personification riddle, give each student an object to personify in a riddle. The object can be anything from a paper clip or a rock to a picture frame or a vase. It doesn't have to be a very complicated object, but this activity tends to work better if the objects are completely inanimate. Even using a stuffed dog can be confusing for some students since dogs are alive and can do some things that people do.

Explain that they should try to keep their objects hidden so that no one knows what they are writing about in their riddles. The only rules are that students must use personification to describe their objects and they should not name the object in the riddle since that would give its identity away and ruin the game. Sometimes students need reminders about what personification is. One good example is to use a wire hanger

A Personification Riddle

His hands twist around
before I can catch them,
stop them from turning me old,
always in circles he runs
with my years, hiding memories
behind the *tick tick ticking*
of his brain, red tongue mocking
me as I try to keep up.
What object did I personify? A clock.

Figure 3.2. Teacher example.

to show that the hanger has a neck and shoulders. Students might want to start by deciding whether their objects are girls or boys, which usually makes students think of their objects in human terms. Then ask them how the objects might have body parts, actions, and emotions. This should get them started.

After the class has had time to finish their riddles, ask for volunteers to share. If there is time, it is fun to have every student participate. Each time a student reads his or her riddle, the class gets three chances to guess what the object is. Right after they guess the object, ask the class to give one or two examples of personification used in the riddle. By the time they have all shared, most, if not all, students should have a good grasp on what personification is and how to use it. Two student examples are shown below.

Personification: Bike Lock
Alan

His arms reach to come together
Keeping whatever he has in his
grasp safe. He has his own
code to follow to confuse
others so they won't take
away what he has in his
grasp.

Personification: Coffee in a Cup
Sheila

It's soft in my hand as it pulls out its blanket to keep my brain warm. Its walls know when we are cold, but it can't do anything about it. It comes with me to school or work. When I am sleepy, it nudges me and I wake up. It's like my body, knowing when it needs to heat up. It whispers to me that the day has begun.

Reading: Identifying the Person

Once again, by the end of this lesson students should be able to define personification, identify it in a poem, use it in their own writing, and explain how it affects the meaning of a piece of writing. In other words, students will go through most of Bloom's taxonomy.

Before reading the following poems, take a moment to ask students if they know what the words *mi madre* and *luna* mean since they are written in Spanish in the poems. If no one knows what these terms mean, write them on the board and have a volunteer look up their meanings in an English/Spanish dictionary and record their translations on the board.

Classroom Snapshot: Most of my students already knew what these words mean because many of them are around Spanish speakers or they themselves speak Spanish at home with their families. Giving English language learners a reason to use their native language in the classroom is a great way to motivate them to participate and see this poetry as relevant.

I also spent a few minutes talking about the herbs listed in the poem "Mi Madre" since many students had not heard of manzanilla or dormilon. We discussed the medicinal qualities of these herbs, where they grow, and how they are used. This was important once we had read the poem and discussed why the desert was like a mother to the speaker. I found quite a bit of information on manzanilla on the Web site http://www.abroadviewmagazine.com/regions/lat_amer/manz_med.html.

The poem "Mi Madre" is the best one to start with because the personification is so obvious. In every other line, Mora describes the desert as a nurturing mother. While reading this poem, it is fun to have students raise their hands every time they spot personification being used instead of having them underline the examples they find since there are so many of them.

Mi Madre

I say feed me.
She serves red prickly pears on a spiked cactus.

I say tease me.
She sprinkles raindrops in my face on a sunny day.

I say frighten me.
She shouts thunder, flashes lightning.

I say comfort me.
She invites me to lay on her firm body.

I say heal me.
She gives me *manzanilla, orégano, dormilón.*

I say caress me.
She strokes my skin with her warm breath.

I say make me beautiful.
She offers turquoise for my fingers, a pink blossom for my hair.

I say sing to me.
She chants lonely women's songs of femaleness.

I say teach me.
She endures: glaring heat
                numbing cold
                frightening dryness.

She: the desert
She: strong mother.

"Luna, Luna" is another beautiful example of personification, but it is much more complicated than "Mi Madre." This poem is a bit more confusing because the moon is referred to as "it" in the first stanza while later in the poem the moon is "her." Also, none of the examples of personification are as overt as they are in "Mi Madre." For example, in the middle of the poem the moon hypnotizes the speaker, and toward the end the speaker peels away flesh from the moon, but neither of these examples of personification jump out at students as readily as when the desert sang lonely women's songs in "Mi Madre." For this reason, it is a good idea to read this poem twice, ask students to underline the examples they find, and have a thorough discussion of how the moon is being personified before leaving this poem.

Luna, Luna

I slice the moon quickly
for it tugs to slip away,
to glide back on its beams.

On nights white with her fullness
I sit alone deep in the desert

away from noisy lights
hearing wise wind, lone owls
until she hypnotizes me again
and all is white blaze.
My arms reach to her, my fingertips
stretch to draw her, draw her
into my lap, only for a moment
while I peel a pale host before she
slides away. I slice the moist
sweet flesh into slivers, store the glow
in a cloth bag. I feed it to women
sad with their bodies. Some nights
I taste *la luna* myself, my lids shut
as she drifts through me
opens my eyes.

Once students have a good understanding of both poems, give them the organizer in Figure 3.3. Explain that the purpose of this exercise is to show that students understand how personification is being used in the two poems above. They should be able to answer the following question: Why did Mora use personification in this way to describe these things?

Extension

Personification Relays

Have students get into two lines, creating two teams, and place an object at the front of the room. Explain that the goal is for each team, one person at a time, to come up with as many ways to personify the object and to write the personification on the board before the timer goes off. The first few times, students may need more time than they will need later when they get used to the game. Allow each team to elect one team member to be a life line in case someone on the team needs a little prompting. This is a fun way to bring literary devices to kinesthetic learners.

Theme: The Shoebox Poem

If you asked your class to tell you in one sentence or less what the Harry Potter books are about, I would be willing to bet that most of them would come up with some sort of thematic statement. "They're about a boy trying to be a wizard." "They're about good versus evil." "Harry Potter is the hero's journey."

Theme is a fun concept to teach because it has to do with recognizing patterns, and students are generally pretty good at figuring out

Name_____

Personification

Directions: In the left column, list three human characteristics from each poem. In the right column, compare the human characteristics with the object being described (desert or moon). Use complete sentences in the right column.

"Mi Madre"	
Human Characteristics	Compared to the desert
Example: "She serves red prickly pears on a spiked cactus."	The desert "serves" prickly pears by providing the soil for cactus to grow the prickly pears.
"She strokes my skin with her warm breath."	The air in the desert is warm, just like a breath.
"She gives me manzanilla, oregano, dormilon."	The desert grows herbs and spices.
"She sprinkles raindrops in my face on a sunny day."	It sometimes rains in the desert, even on sunny days.
"Luna, Luna"	
Human Characteristics	Compared to the moon
"she hypnotizes me again"	The moon hypnotizes people by its beauty, light, and fullness.
"she / slides away"	The moon slides away by setting and having the sun take her place.
"as she drifts through me / opens my eyes."	The moonlight goes through your eyes and makes you want to keep looking at it.

Directions: In complete sentences, explain why you think Pat Mora decided to personify the desert and the moon in these poems. Use textual evidence to explain your answer.

I believe she personified these objects because in real life they make her feel better and they are important to her. She feels that the desert is a guiding and loving presence because she referred to it as her mother. She says that she sometimes eats the moon to heal herself. She feels that the moon gives female empowerment because she gives it to other women to feel better about themselves. She needed to make the desert and the moon seem more real, like they are her friends.

Figure 3.3. Student answers (answers will vary depending on examples chosen).

what ideas are in common in works of literature as long as they are not asked to be too abstract too soon. One way to do this is to have students find themes through a brainstorming activity.

Reading: Sticky Note Rotation

The goal of the *sticky note rotation* is to see how much students can get from a poem without any prompting. Start by reading all three of the following poems aloud or by having a volunteer read, and instead of starting with discussion, place three big sticky notes on the walls around the classroom, and write the title of one poem on each of them. Tape up a copy of the poem that corresponds with each piece of paper so students can easily read while they are discussing. Then, put students in groups of three or four and explain that there are no wrong answers at this stage of the activity. The only goal is for students to work together to brainstorm words that describe the main ideas of the poems and to write new words on the sticky notes as it is their turn. Give all groups a few minutes to collaborate before telling them that it's time, and then give each group sixty seconds to write as many words as they can to answer the following questions:

- What is the poem about?
- What is being said about life in this poem?

After the initial sixty seconds, signal that it's time for groups to rotate to the next sticky note and repeat the activity with the other two poems. By the time all groups have rotated through, all students should have contributed at least one new word to the wall for each poem, creating a brainstorm list of possible themes for the three poems in this section.

Now is when some answers become more appropriate than others, but instead of eliminating the "wrong" answers from the walls, circle the answers that students agree with so that they are making the decisions. Have a volunteer go to the board to make a list of words that are written on more than one list, showing where patterns occur. At this point, it's a good idea for students to have the poems in front of them so they can support their choices with textual evidence.

In Mora's poem "Teenagers," the speaker describes what it is like to watch his or her children turn into teenagers. The speaker is just an observer with no real control over what is happening. The children that used to be small have disappeared and reappeared as pseudoadults. Some of the themes that students might find in this poem are as follows:

- Puberty
- Losing control
- Growing up
- Forgetting how to talk to kids once they turn into teenagers
- Change

Teenagers

One day they disappear
into their rooms.
Doors and lips shut
and we become strangers
in our own home.

I pace the hall, hear whispers,
a code I knew but can't remember,
mouthed by mouths I taught to speak.

Years later the door opens.
I see faces I once held,
open as sunflowers in my hands. I see
familiar skin now stretched on long bodies
that move past me
glowing almost like pearls.

"Same Song" is that familiar story of the awkwardness children feel as they are trying to fit into their bodies. The son and daughter in this poem seem to want to fit in, but they are not sure what it takes, which is why they work so hard and still frown at themselves at the end of the day. Some of the themes found in this poem are as follows:

- Trying to figure out who you are
- Trying to fit in
- Learning your role in society—girls are supposed to be pretty, boys are supposed to be strong
- Change
- Growing up

Same Song

While my sixteen-year-old son sleeps,
my twelve-year-old daughter
stumbles into the bathroom at six a.m.
plugs in the curling iron
squeezes into faded jeans
curls her hair carefully
strokes Aztec Blue shadow on her eyelids
smoothes Frosted Mauve blusher on her cheeks

outlines her mouth in Neon Pink
peers into the mirror, mirror on the wall
frowns at her face, her eyes, her skin,
not fair.

At night this daughter
stumbles off to bed at nine
eyes half-shut while my son
jogs a mile in the cold dark
then lifts weights in the garage
curls and bench presses
expanding biceps, triceps, pectorals,
one-handed push-ups, one hundred sit-ups
peers into that mirror, mirror and frowns too.

for Libby

The poem "Disguise" looks at the issue of growing up from a slightly different perspective. The speaker seems to want to go back in time to when she could still fit in her grandmother's lap, back when she did not have to "smear on make-up every day" (*Borders* 12). In many ways the speaker in this poem parallels the daughter in "Same Song" since they are both making themselves up for the world. Some themes for this poem might be as follows:

- Wearing a mask
- Wanting to not be a grownup
- Missing childhood
- Looking back
- Trying to figure out where you fit—"in my grandmother's lap" (7)
- Practicing your role in society

Disguise

Gold heels and a long purple dress
strut down the hall on a spring afternoon
  Grown Up
        until I stepped out
of the heavy clothes left in a pile
red-red lipstick on top, the real me curled
in my grandmother's lap.

Black heels and a proper gray dress
walk down the hall on a fall afternoon
  Grown Up
        I stand on tiptoes in there
to smear on make-up every day walk
stilt legs on thin heels, daydream
of shedding this heavy skin, fitting
in a steady lap.

After students have narrowed the words down and discussed the things that the poems have in common, work with the class to write a thematic statement for the three poems. Start by deciding what the main topic is of all three poems. Then figure out what Pat Mora is saying about life. What observations is she making? Some possible thematic statements are as follows:

- Growing up is difficult whether you're going through it or just watching someone else go through it.
- No matter where we are in life, sometimes we'd rather be somewhere else.
- Finding yourself is hard even when you're looking straight in a mirror.

Activity: Theme Box Poems

Now that students have read the poems several times and have created thematic statements for them, they are ready to create theme box poems. Have them bring in shoeboxes and old magazines that they do not mind cutting up. Their goal is to collect words and images from the magazines that match the theme of these poems.

Since shoeboxes have an inside and an outside, ask students to choose images to put on the outside of the box that show what growing up looks like to the outside world. They can use the inside of the box to show what it feels like to grow up. It is okay for students to share magazines and other materials during this activity, but because of its personal nature most students feel more comfortable working beside, not with, their classmates.

Once they have covered their shoeboxes with images, students are ready to write their own poems about growing up, using the images on the box as a guide. Start by asking a student to volunteer to share some of the images on his or her box. While recording these images on the board, discuss with the class ways in which they might turn this into a poem. One way for students to get started is to write a list poem of all the things on the shoebox. They can add better detail and description to the list when they are satisfied that they have included everything from the box that is important to them. This is an easy way to take students from prewriting (finding images in magazines) to rough draft (list poems) to revision (adding details) without them feeling like they are rewriting the same thing again and again.

No More Lilacs
Olivia

When I was born
they planted lilacs
outside my window
and every year
the bloom caught my nose
by surprise
every year it was the same
purple breeze that blew
me into summer –
one year older.

Now I live in a new house
with green bushes and rocks
growing outside my window.
They always look the same
even though everything else
is changing all the time.

I wish I could find a lilac bush
to prove it's summer again
to see the tiny blossoms looking
up at me so I know I'm not alone.

Extension

Thematic Photographs

Ask your class to bring in several photographs that show them at different ages, and have them think about what the pictures have in common. How were they the same at age two as they were at age five or ten? How have they changed? Are there any patterns to the ways they have changed? Have each student brainstorm themes for his or her series of pictures and write a story or poem making an observation about his or her life by describing the photos in detail.

4 Interdisciplinary Connections

Three of my friends—one a PhD candidate in literature, one a humanities teacher, and the other an engineer—all have one thing in common: a love of nature, rivers in particular. The literature student uses philosophy and literary theory as a foundation for studying and writing about rivers. The humanities teacher looks at rivers in a social and historical context, asking about human responsibility to rivers and how we can serve them in productive and environmentally friendly ways. The engineer utilizes calculus to create formulas to understand how rivers affect land and other parts of the environment.

Another group of friends at Colorado State University recently collaborated to create an art/poetry show that featured text as art and visual art as poetry. The show's opening presented art and poetry on the walls, but also poetry readings, modern dance, a short play, and live music. The goal was to bring together as many forms of art as possible and to see how collaboration between different genres might create new brilliance.

We live in an interdisciplinary world that is constantly pushing us to cross lines. The classroom should be no different. This chapter features the poetry of Giovanni, Lee, and Mora, respectively, as part of three interdisciplinary lessons. Nikki Giovanni's poem, "The Funeral of Martin Luther King, Jr." is paired with Dr. King's "I Have a Dream" speech in a history lesson about the civil rights movement. The poem "Mnemonic" is the centerpiece of the Li-Young Lee section where students learn about the way memory functions in the brain in a biology lesson. The last section presents an art lesson using Pat Mora's poem, "Still Life." All of these are project-based lessons that require more than one class period to complete, but the multiple levels of learning that they necessitate are well worth the extra time.

Entering History: Nikki Giovanni and Civil Rights

In 1968, the year of Martin Luther King Jr.'s assassination, Nikki Giovanni was twenty-five years old. During that year, she dropped out of graduate school and wrote most of what would become her second volume of poetry, *Black Feeling, Black Talk, Black Judgement*, which includes the following poem, a reaction to what she saw at Dr. King's funeral in Atlanta, Georgia.

The Funeral of Martin Luther King, Jr.

His headstone read
FREE AT LAST, FREE AT LAST
But death is a slave's freedom
We seek the freedom of free men
And the construction of a world
Where Martin Luther King could have lived
and preached non-violence

In the quest to make poetry relevant to middle school students, it is important to take them out of their own lives in order to help them understand the magnitude of historical events and how those events still affect us today. This short yet powerful poem does just that. In seven lines, Nikki Giovanni manages to create a setting (the headstone), give the readers a quote from the headstone and from Dr. King's "I Have a Dream" speech ("FREE AT LAST, FREE AT LAST"), and include commentary about what she thinks of this tribute to one of the most influential leaders of all time.

This poem gives language arts teachers the opportunity to teach using two forms of literary criticism, intertextuality and new historicism, as the framework for their lesson. Intertextuality is the practice of studying one piece of literature in relation to another, and new historicism allows a reader to take a literary work and study it in a historical context. Giovanni's line, "FREE AT LAST, FREE AT LAST," links her poem directly to Dr. King's speech, which in turn naturally leads to a study of the history behind the speech and King's death. This section allows students to read a poem using its place in history as a tool rather than just relying on the poem itself to convey meaning. Studying these two texts together is a valuable way to incorporate social studies and literature, specifically the civil rights movement and the life of Martin Luther King Jr.

Readers' Theater

In order to teach middle school students a text like Dr. King's "I Have a Dream" speech that is so full of historical references and figurative language, it is a good idea to break it down into palatable chunks so that students are not overwhelmed. The speech can be divided up by number of lines or by paragraphs, depending on the number of students there are. It is also important to test students' understanding of the text using more than one type of assessment. In this lesson, a student-generated quiz, readers' theater, and reflective writing are used to accomplish this goal. Readers' theater is a strategy often used to show students how to give voice to a text and to engage reluctant readers. It usually involves a group reading from a text without memorizing it or using props. For this speech, it is important that students have a good understanding of the text before asking them to read it aloud.

Start by playing the recording that has Dr. King's own voice delivering the speech in Washington while students read along. Allowing students to hear Dr. King's speech given live not only puts the speech into context, but it gives students a chance to hear the way it originally sounded. Ask students to focus on the way Dr. King uses his voice to evoke emotion and place emphasis on specific words. After listening to the speech, allow the class to ask clarifying questions to make sure they understand who King's audience was and what his purpose was in writing such an unforgettable speech. Also, give students a few minutes to underline words that they do not know or phrases such as "Emancipation Proclamation" that have to do with history. (Note: The recording of "I Have a Dream" can be found at many public libraries, and the written copy of the speech can be located at the following website: http://www.americanrhetoric.com/speeches/Ihaveadream. htm.)

Give each student the organizer in Figure 4.1 to record the words and phrases they underlined. Students will then research their words and phrases in order to complete the organizer. It is important to talk to students about the difference between the meaning of a word or phrase and the way it is used in the context of Dr. King's speech. This is an opportunity to talk about the denotations and connotations of words. Once students have a better understanding of what their sections of the speech mean, they should be able to do two things: write paragraphs explaining their sections of the speech and formulate quiz questions that will test the knowledge of the rest of the class. Allow students to share and discuss their questions with the whole class so that students will have a chance to ask questions and take notes before being quizzed on their understanding of the speech.

Classroom Snapshot: Below are some example quiz questions that my students wrote. My class recorded their questions on a piece of butcher paper that had been divided into two columns, one for questions and one for answers. Every day that we worked on the speech, I gave students a few minutes at the beginning of class to write answers on the wall. This was our way of reviewing for the quiz that came at the very end of this lesson. Ultimately, I wanted to see that my students could accurately define words and explain phrases using the context of the speech and historical information to support their answers.

- What does "in whose symbolic shadow we stand" mean?
- What is the Declaration of Independence?
- What does Martin Luther King mean by "a bad check which has come back marked insufficient funds"?
- What does this sentence mean? "The whirlwind of revolt will continue to share the foundations of our nation until the bright day of justice emerges."
- What was Dr. King trying to say when he said, "together at a table of brotherhood"?
- Who was the Governor of Alabama when this speech was given and how did he change as a person after he was governor?

Now that students have a better idea of what the speech means, they are ready to prepare for readers' theater. There are several ways to conduct readers' theater, but for this lesson the goal is for students to perform their parts of Dr. King's speech in their own, unique ways and to combine their sections so that, in the end, the speech is read in full. For their sections, students should decide who will read what lines, which words or phrases will be read by more than one person simultaneously, and what tone of voice will be used to express different emotions. For example, toward the middle of the speech, the phrases "go back" and "I have a dream" are repeated several times. The whole class might want to read those lines or girls and boys might want to alternate to create different voices.

Once all of the students are ready, rehearse the speech several times before performing it in front of a real audience. One way to give students a chance to ask questions and give feedback is to have the class become the audience. Explain that when students are not performing, they will act as an audience that is allowed to ask questions and give warm and cool feedback after each performance. Warm feedback consists of encouraging comments about the performance, and cool feedback is constructive advice on how to improve the performance. Have each student or group of students perform their part in the correct order, stopping between sections to answer questions and receive feedback. Continue to rehearse until students feel confident enough to perform in front of a new audience.

I Have a Dream

Directions: Use the space below to write your section of the speech. This will help you become more familiar with the speech and will make the speech easily accessible while you define the words and phrases from your section.

I am happy to join with you today in what will go down in history as the greatest demonstration for freedom in the history of our nation.

Five **score** years ago, **a great American**, in whose symbolic shadow we stand, signed the **Emancipation Proclamation**. This momentous **decree** came as a great beacon light of hope to millions of Negro slaves who had been **seared in the flames of withering injustice**. It came as a joyous daybreak to end the long night of captivity. But one hundred years later, we must face the tragic fact that the Negro is still not free.

One hundred years later, the life of the Negro is still sadly crippled by the **manacles** of segregation and the chains of discrimination.

Directions: Use the space below to record information about the words and/or phrases from your section of the speech. List the words and/or phrases in the left column, record the meanings you found through research in the middle column, and explain what the words and/or phrases mean in the context of Martin Luther King Jr.'s speech in the right column.

Word/Phrase from Speech	Definition	Meaning in Context
Score	twenty years	Dr. King is explaining that the Emancipation Proclamation was signed 100 years ago.
a great American	Abraham Lincoln	He is the President who signed the Emancipation Proclamation.
Emancipation Proclamation	the document that freed the slaves in 1862	Dr. King opens his speech by mentioning the Emancipation Proclamation to show that, even though "Negroes" are no longer slaves, they are still not free.
decree	a lawful order	Dr. King is saying that the Emancipation Proclamation gave hope to slaves by making slavery illegal.
seared in the flames of withering injustice	burning in a fire caused by injustice	Dr. King is saying that slavery has hurt African American people and *continued on next page*

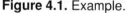
Figure 4.1. Example.

Figure 4.1. continued

		that the justice or fairness got smaller and smaller in America during slavery.
manacles	something that confines or binds, especially the hands	Dr. King is using the analogy of binding the hands of "Negroes" to describe how segregation affects them.

Directions: Use the space below to write a paragraph explaining what your section of the speech is saying. Explain it so that your classmates will have a clearer idea of what the speech means when you share your paragraph.

Dr. King is welcoming his audience and acknowledging the fact that the March on Washington was to go down in history as a great demonstration of freedom. He is talking about how things such as the Emancipation Proclamation, signed by Abraham Lincoln, that were supposed to create freedom and equality for African Americans haven't worked as well as they should have. The Emancipation Proclamation ended slavery but did not end segregation and discrimination.

Performing a readers' theater in front of an audience is a great way to publish student work. Invite parents for an after-school performance; perform for another grade in your school, or go into the community and invite people who may be interested in Martin Luther King Jr. or civil rights to watch your students perform.

Reflecting on the Experience

Now that students are familiar with Dr. King's "I Have a Dream" speech, give them Nikki Giovanni's poem and discuss her reaction to the inscription on the headstone at Dr. King's funeral. Talk about the meaning of the word *freedom* and how Giovanni uses it in her poem. Then, give students three different ways to reflect on their experiences with these texts.

Martin Luther King Jr. in Today's World

Ask students to focus on the last four lines of Giovanni's poem: "We seek the freedom of free men/ And the construction of a world/ Where Martin Luther King could have lived/ and preached non-violence" (4–7). Have students write about whether or not they believe Martin Luther King Jr. could live and preach nonviolence in today's world. They should support their opinions with evidence from what they have learned about

the civil rights movement, examples of current events, and their understanding of the word *freedom*.

Martin Luther King, Jr. in Today's World
Armand

How does our modern culture accept difference? How would they
accept Dr. King? What if Dr. King lived today and had preached
to this world?

I believe that his reception would be met with support, but
also with a lot of resentment.

Let us say Dr. King returned to us today in, oh, how about
Cincinnati, Ohio. If he returned to that city, where there are still
race riots, racist cops, and racial injustice, would his vision, his
dream, be accomplished? Or would he still have to fight for freedom, still use peace rallies, his nonviolent protests? Or, perhaps,
in this unforgiving environment of modern day "civilization,"
he would have to resort to a different kind of protest, perhaps
more like Malcolm X.

The first eight years of my life I lived in Cincinnati, Ohio, a
city which is still plagued by "the manacles of segregation and
the chains of discrimination." Not long ago, riots clogged the city
and there is still much violence and racial tension. If Dr. King
went to Cincinnati, he would probably be met with violence in a
world where that is all we know. Dr. King's peaceful protest and
nonviolence is almost like ancient history, so used are we to the
thought of solving our problems with violence. Many of us think
that our problems with racism are through, but they aren't, and if
Dr. King could see where his valiant efforts have gotten the African American community, he would probably shake his head like
a disappointed father. His efforts weren't in vain though because
African Americans do have much more freedom and are treated
equally and like people, like the people they are and have been
for as long as anyone.

Freedom is not just being free from having a slave owner or
not being chained to a stone wall with manacles of iron. No one
is truly free, but why must we all be held captive by fear of one
another? Isn't this what the good Doctor was saying the whole
time? We are all equal, and equality is nothing to fear. The arro-
gance of superiority is, however, and the ruthlessness of tyranny
should be terrifying. If we could all be free of fear and of hate and
accept each other as brothers, sisters, and friends, we may then
get somewhere.

I think if Dr. King were here today he would still fight back
without raising a hand against anyone. I think if he was alive
today he would still fight for freedom, for all, from the chains
which hold us, binding us to our disgusting beliefs. I believe that
he would keep going until the end as he did before, and this time,
it will be the majority who is outnumbered.

Writing as Nikki Giovanni

Ask students to imagine that Nikki Giovanni was in Washington in 1963 to hear Dr. King's speech. How would she have reacted to his speech? How would it have made her feel? What would she have written about it? Students must put themselves in the place of Nikki Giovanni and write a reflection about the experience of hearing Dr. King's speech from her point of view. It can be in the form of a letter, journal entry, or poem.

> **August 28, 1963**
> *Jenny*
>
> I saw a million birds today reaching for the sky with clipped wings. All of them fluttering toward the voice of Dr. King, and I was standing like a stone in the middle of it all, frozen in awe. His voice was a deep drum full of promise, so full that it was overflowing onto the frantic birds until they stopped panicking and sang. Things are changing. The air is thick with it, and all I want to do is inhale as deeply as possible. All I want to do is fly.

Agents of Change

Ask students to write a letter to a politician, a modern-day civil rights activist, or a newspaper explaining what needs to change in your community or in America in order for Martin Luther King Jr.'s dream to be realized. You may want to start by brainstorming a list of actions with the class that may promote positive change. Tell students that they should focus on one thing they think should be changed and explain why and how making that change will help your community or our country become more tolerant of differences.

> Dear New York Times,
>
>   In 1963, Martin Luther King, Jr. gave his amazing "I Have a Dream" speech to try and change the course of racism in the U.S. Forty-one years later there is a new kind of racism, racist jokes among the young community.
>
>   Rude nicknames and names based on race and stereotypes include "white trash" and the "N" word. These are all offensive and I hear all these words a lot from my peers, not as insults but as jokes. When people tell these kinds of jokes, it makes them look like racists. It's not that people are born racist, but they learn it in school, from parents, from friends, from TV, anywhere. I personally think that we should not teach racism by telling racist jokes or by listening to them.
>
>   I propose that people take a stand against these jokes that can be extremely offensive and have a negative effect on our community. Whenever you hear someone tell a joke that could be hurtful, tell them to stop or walk away so they know it's not funny.

Once this happens, these people might start to think before they tell racist jokes. Do you want this kind of bad humor in our community? Take a stand today!

Sincerely,
Laura and Flip

Extensions

I have often had students become intrigued, obsessed even, with subjects such as the Holocaust or a president's assassination when we have read something related to those subjects, and I always want to give those students more, make time to explore further. Unfortunately, there is rarely time to stop everything to continue with a subject that we may have already devoted several days or weeks to, but it is always a good idea to have literature available in the event that students ask for more.

There are two texts written by Martin Luther King Jr. that may be of particular interest to students. The first is the speech he gave the day before he was assassinated in 1968 called "I See the Promised Land." The second is the letter he wrote to clergymen while he was in the Birmingham jail in 1963 ("Letter"). These pieces offer a great deal of historical context that students will want (and probably need) to research as they read.

Many of Nikki Giovanni's poems are related to the civil rights movement, but there are three in particular that could be paired with Dr. King's texts. All three of the poems can be found in the "Black Feeling Black Talk/Black Judgment" section of *The Selected Poems of Nikki Giovanni*. They are called "Poem (No Name No. 3)," "Poem for Black Boys (With Special Love to James)," and "The Great Pax Whitie." Some of these poems use charged and racial language that may be offensive to some readers, so be sure to frontload with students the reasons and context in which Giovanni may have used such language before you let them go on their own with it.

Discovering Memory: Poetry and Science

Memory is an important tool for poets. We store away what life gives us and hope that it comes back in some form that will be worthy of reaching the page, but sometimes what memory does is perplexing. It stirs around in the brain and shoots out from synapses that turn memories different colors and shapes. Sometimes we remember the same way we dream—in black and white, with the sound off, filled with faceless characters whose names we should know—and sometimes we don't remember at all. Li-Young Lee's poem, "Mnemonic," tells of the speaker's struggle to understand how his memory works and ultimately to remember his father.

In this lesson, students learn about memory by doing a memory writing exercise, studying the brain to understand how it affects memory, reading Lee's poem "Mnemonic," and creating projects to demonstrate their new understanding of memory.

Prereading: Memory Lists

Start by writing words on the board that will spark students' memories, and ask them to start making a memory list as soon as they see a word that reminds them of something. Explain that the list does not have to make sense and all the words do not have to relate to one another. For example, the words *roller coaster* can lead to *cotton candy*, which can lead to *pink tongue* and *headache* and *sleeping in the car* and *seat belts* and *pillows* and *twinkling stars* and so on. The point is to allow one thing to lead to another and see where it goes.

Once students have the opportunity to brainstorm a good memory list, ask them to read through it and circle the five most important or interesting words or phrases in the list. On a separate piece of paper, have students incorporate those words or phrases into a larger piece of writing. It can be either a poem or story, but ultimately it should use their memories to bring an experience closer to them and to the reader. Give volunteers a chance to share their writing and discuss what their memories mean to them and why they used the words and phrases they did to bring the memories to life.

> *Cameron*
> The five words/phrases I used are *snowball fight*, *Kansas*, *fort*, *pain*, and *hiding*.
>
> **Winter in Kansas**
>
> Crisp frozen air beat us down
> six of us working together
> in the snow, a Kansas winter
> gifted us enough of the solid white stuff
> to make a fort, a refuge from the war
> we were planning.
>
> "Snowball fight!"
> The signal was yelled
> and we all went into hiding,
> three on a side with steam engines pumping
> out of our noses and mouths.
>
> Ice bullets flew from every direction.
> "Bam! Bam! Bam!" My brother screamed,

throwing a snowball from each hand.
I was hit, shot with a cold pain that broke through
three layers of clothes.

Our war lasted for hours.
Brothers, sister, and neighborhood friends
recruited to die on the field before
going inside for hot chocolate and cartoons.

Classroom Snapshot: When I asked students to share their memory pieces, I was most interested in helping them understand how their memories developed. How did Cameron, the student who wrote "Winter in Kansas," remember details about the day she had a snowball fight in Kansas? What kinds of memories were most vivid to them? Most of the students in my class said that they remembered things best that affected them emotionally. For example, one of my students wrote about the day he broke his arm, while someone else wrote about the best birthday present she ever received. I wanted my students to think about why they might be more apt to remember something like what it was like getting their first pets rather than what they learned in one of their classes in elementary school. This discussion easily led to the next activity—learning about how memory works in the brain.

Research: Learning about the Brain

Start by showing students the following Web site—www.explora torium.edu/memory/—and giving them a few minutes to click around and learn a little bit about the brain in relation to memory. Once they have had a chance to look at the Web site freely, put the questions in Figure 4.2 on an overhead and have students work in groups of three or four to answer the questions on paper. Most of the answers can be found in the section of the Web site called "Sheep Brain Dissection" and other parts of the Exploratorium Web site, but students may have to search other sites to learn about mnemonic devices.

Once the class has compiled as much as they can about how memory works in the brain, they are ready to read the poem "Mnemonic."

Reading: Filling in the Gaps

In Li-Young Lee's poem "Mnemonic," the speaker remembers a moment when his father gave him a blue sweater to keep him warm. He remem-

- What are the three different types of memory?
  - ◆ Working memory, long-term memory, and skill memory
- Which parts of the brain are responsible for each type of memory?
  - ◆ Working memory occurs in the prefrontal cortex. Long-term memory is kept in the hippocampus. Skill memory is in the cerebellum.
- What are some problems with memory? (Answers may vary.)
  - ◆ Sometimes people remember events differently from the way they really happened.
  - ◆ People sometimes remember things that didn't really happen.
  - ◆ Things like stress and sleep deprivation can cause memory loss.
- What are mnemonic devices?
  - ◆ Mnemonic devices are ways to help people remember things such as lists, the order of operations, or vocabulary in a foreign language.
- Why do mnemonic devices work?
  - ◆ Mnemonic devices work because they help break complicated information into more manageable pieces. They connect prior knowledge to new knowledge helping the brain to make sense of information it has never seen before.

Figure 4.2. Brain questions and answers.

bers other bits and pieces of information about his father, like the fact that he was a serious man with a good memory and that he would be ashamed of the speaker because his memory has no order.

While reading this poem with the class, ask them to think about what they have learned about the brain. Is the speaker using long- or short-term memory? Is he using the hippocampus, cerebellum, or the prefrontal cortex? How do you know? Ask students to work individually or in small groups to underline the parts of the poem that indicate some sort of memory and label those lines with a part of the brain. Students should be able to explain their answers using textual evidence and/or information they gathered from the Exploratorium Web site.

Mnemonic

I was tired. So I lay down.
My lids grew heavy. So I slept.
Slender memory, stay with me.[1]

---

1. This seems to be a long-term memory because the speaker wants it to stay with him. It would be in the hippocampus. (Alex)

I was cold once. So my father took off his blue sweater.

He wrapped me in it, and I never gave it back.
It is the sweater he wore to America,
this one, which I've grown into, whose sleeves are too long,
whose elbows have thinned, who outlives its rightful owner.
Flamboyant blue in daylight, poor blue by daylight,
it is black in the folds.[2]

A serious man who devised complex systems of numbers and
    rhymes
to aid him in remembering, a man who forgot nothing,[3] my
    father
would be ashamed of me.
Not because I'm forgetful,
but because there is no order
to my memory, a heap
of details, uncatalogued, illogical.[4]
For instance:
God was lonely. So he made me.

My father loved me. So he spanked me.
It hurt him to do so. He did it daily.[5]

The earth is flat. Those who fall off don't return.
The earth is round. All things reveal themselves to men only
    gradually.

I won't last. Memory is sweet.
Even when it's painful, memory is sweet.

Once I was cold. So my father took off his blue sweater.

After students have had a chance to label different lines from the poem, ask them to share their answers as a class. This is a good time to

---

2. I think this memory was triggered by the blue sweater because he says "this one" like he's wearing it while he's thinking. If that's true, then this memory is in the prefrontal cortex. Working memory takes things that have been stored in the brain, probably in the hippocampus, and brings them up when one of the senses causes them to be triggered. (Veronica)
3. The father used mnemonic devices to help him remember things. Mnemonic devices help working memory in the prefrontal cortex. They store information in the working memory until it's ready to become a long-term memory and go to the hippocampus. (Charlie)
4. I think this is describing the hippocampus because long-term memories are the most disorganized. The website we looked at talked about how people usually remember things wrong, especially when they happened a long time ago. The speaker is trying to remember his father, but he can only remember pieces of him. (Robin)
5. This would have to be a long-term memory in the hippocampus because the speaker's father is dead and can't spank him anymore. Plus, I think the speaker is an adult because he's talking about his father in past tense. (Isa)

discuss the poem together to help students discover how this poem might be a mnemonic device in itself. How might the speaker or Lee be using this poem to remember his father? Does it work? Why or why not?

Classroom Snapshot: I used this discussion time with my class to relate the poem "Mnemonic" to the memory pieces my students wrote at the beginning of this lesson. I passed students' writing out to them and asked them to compare their memories to those that Lee wrote about in his poem. Most students realized that if they wrote about events that happened a long time ago they were less likely to remember details, while those students who wrote about a pet that they still owned or a place they had just visited were able to describe it much more accurately. From this, students were able to conclude that the speaker in "Mnemonic" still had the sweater that his father gave him because he described it in great detail, but they thought the father probably died a long time ago since the speaker could not remember as much about him as he could about the sweater.

Activity: Representing Memory in the Brain

Now that students have learned some basic information about how memory works in the brain and have related that information to Lee's poem, it's time for them to use what they know about memory to create something new. Put students into groups of three or four and ask each group to choose a product from the lists below. Groups should sign up for one of the categories to make sure everyone is not making similar things. Ultimately, it works best to see two or three products from each category in the classroom at the end of the project.

- Informational: brochure, PowerPoint, poster, research paper, pamphlet, public service announcement . . .
- Creative: sculpture, drawing, painting, game, diagram . . .
- Personal: poem, story, letter, photography with captions . . .

The goal of this activity is for students to create something that shows what they have learned about memory and the brain. Students should use the brain questions that they answered earlier as a guide while working on their products. For example, students might make a brochure informing people about the causes of memory loss. They might also create a diagram or a clay model to show the different parts of the brain that are responsible for memory, or they could write a poem describing a mnemonic device that works for them.

Internet Note: The Exploratorium Memory Exhibition Web site that students were introduced to earlier has several features that will assist them in their projects. Besides having a diagram of the brain with descriptions of different parts relating to memory, the site also includes "Lecture Series Webcasts" about a range of memory-related topics such as how stress affects memory and how children's memories are different from adults' memories. Students will also enjoy playing with Droodles, a combination of riddles and doodles, to test their own memories.

Classroom Snapshot: When I taught this lesson, I required that students incorporate Li-Young Lee's poem "Mnemonic" into their products. For some students this worked well, and for others it was frustrating. One group sculpted a brain out of clay and, instead of just labeling the parts of the brain, they also included different stanzas from the poem to show where in the brain these memories were stored. This was a creative and successful project, but another group decided to act out a public service announcement about stress-related memory loss, and they could not find a good way to integrate the poem into their idea. It turned out that the groups whose products were informational had the most trouble including "Mnemonic," but most students who chose creative or personal products were able to incorporate the poem. My greatest concerns were that students understand both the poem and what we had studied about memory, but since "Mnemonic" was discussed thoroughly before students started working on their projects, I felt assured that both of these goals were met.

Extension

Organize a Memory Fair

In the spirit of making projects like this one as authentic as possible, give your students an audience by helping them organize a memory fair. Like a science fair, students can set up their projects in the gym or another open space in your school and prepare to present their work, answering questions about the brain, memory, and how Li-Young Lee's "Mnemonic" applies to what they have produced. Have students collaborate with one another to find classmates who have made things that connect with one another. For example, one group may have made a PowerPoint presentation about how children remember things while another group conducted memory tests with younger siblings. Putting these together will allow students to learn from one another while creating more complicated and thorough projects for the fair.

Artistic Endeavors: Creating a Still Life

Not long ago, I was flipping through Nikki Giovanni's *Cotton Candy on a Rainy Day* and came across a poem called "Fascinations." The last stanza goes like this:

> "if you were a pure bolt
> of fire cutting the skies
> i'd touch you risking my life
> not because i'm brave or strong
> but because i'm fascinated
> by what the outcome will be" (40–45)

I was prompted to paint something to illustrate these lines, an endeavor I'd never attempted before—three blue-purple watercolors cut open by yellow-orange flames. Unsatisfied by any one of the paintings I'd done, I cut them up and put them back together to make one stained glass collage set in a black shadow box topped off with a transparency yielding Giovanni's words, and when I was finished, I couldn't remember which came first, the words or the images. Which was the art? I wasn't sure that it mattered, and to distinguish between the two seemed like a mistake. I gave the piece to a friend as a gift, hoping that ultimately the picture would forget that it was born from words, hoping that it would understand that its real purpose was to frame the world in a new light and become something special for this person. This is the miracle of poetry and art; they seem to bring one another to life, that is, if they can ever really be seen as separate entities.

Pat Mora's poem "Still Life" lends itself to this sort of artistic endeavor, a merging of words into images and back again.

Still Life

Still hearing dawn
alive with birds
stirring the morning breeze.

Still warming my fingers
round a cup, *café* I made
in the quiet
before the world fills the air.

Still opening these doors
heavier now
with my own hands,

weathered brown on brown.

Still holding soles and hammer
mending leather stubborn as my palms
                    gently drumming
                    gently drumming.

Still sweeping slowly as the sun
sets before I walk to the *plaza*
to watch the stars come out,
to watch the girls.

Spring again.

Prereading: Framing the World

To help students understand that a still life is a moment in time, a focused snapshot that analyzes small pieces of the world, it is useful to
practice creating still lifes with them before looking at the poem above.
Start by asking students to take a piece of paper of any size and cut out
the middle to create a frame. I prefer taking students outside for the next
step, but if that is not an option at your school, students can easily complete this activity right in the classroom. Find a good area where each
student can have his or her own space, and ask students to plant themselves in one spot with their frames, something with which to write, and
the organizer in Figure 4.3. Once they are situated, have them place their
frames somewhere that seems interesting to them and leave it there.
(Some students may need to tape their frames to walls, trees, fences, or
the like.) If they can not find an "interesting" place, ask them to find
the most boring space in the area and use that. They will be amazed by
what they find. The goal is to have students focus on the microworld in
their frames and write about it in as much detail as possible.

After students have had time to complete their framing activity,
give them a chance to share with each other. While students read their
descriptions, the class can guess what is being described. Discuss the
importance of detail when trying to describe an image accurately, or
inversely, when trying to imagine words in picture form.

Use the Internet and do a search of the words *still life* with your
students to show them what this category of art has traditionally looked
like. You will find a lot of dishes of fruit and empty furniture in empty
rooms. Focus in on the idea that what the artists are doing is providing
new ways to see ordinary things. Ask students to explain how the still
life art you find is describing the world. How do the artists use details
such as color, shadows, and lines to fully describe the objects? Do they
make the objects bigger or smaller than they would usually be? How
do these techniques affect the way we see and feel about the objects?

Name_____

Framing the World

Directions: Use the space below to draw everything inside your frame to the best of your ability paying close attention to details.

Directions: Write a detailed description of what is inside your frame as if you are trying to describe it to someone who has never seen it before. Be sure to use all of your senses to create as vivid a picture as possible.

Figure 4.3. Graphic organizer.

Reading: Exposing the Images

Now that students have a better understanding of what a still life is, they are ready to read Pat Mora's poem "Still Life" and expose the images in it. Cut the poem into five stanzas, and make enough copies for each student to have one stanza. (The poem is six stanzas long, but since the last stanza is only one line long, it works well to pair it with the next to last stanza for this activity.) Give each student a stanza and unlined paper they can draw on.

After reading the poem aloud the first time, ask students to determine what the most important image is in the stanza they are holding during the second read through. Remind students that Mora is trying to create a certain effect with each of the images she presents in this poem, so finding the right images to draw is of the utmost importance. For example, in the first stanza, "Still hearing dawn / alive with birds / stirring the morning breeze," students must decide whether Mora wants readers to focus on dawn, birds, or the morning breeze. The goal is for students to illustrate their stanzas by making such decisions.

Take it a step further by giving students different materials to work with such as pliable metals (aluminum, pewter, or sheets of gold used to emboss), clay, fabrics, construction paper, or things from outside such as sand, sticks, or leaves and ask them to revise their sketches using these materials. How does this change their snapshot? Has its focus shifted? How does the artwork help to interpret the poem? Students should think about these questions as they create, and at the end of this activity, ask them to write artist statements describing their processes and defending their use of certain materials and techniques. Once all of the stanzas have been illustrated, ask students to put them back together. They need to stay in the order they were originally in, but since there is more than one student per stanza, they can decide how to collect the illustrations. In this way, students will work to construct their own stories and their own interpretations of Mora's poem.

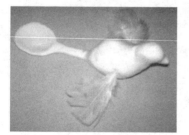

Still hearing dawn
alive with birds
stirring the morning breeze.

Artist Statement for Stanza One:
Kelly

I decided that the most important things in the first stanza were the birds. Since they were "stirring the morning breeze," I made a bird with a spoon for a tail because I wanted my art to represent as much of the stanza as possible. I used Model Magic, feathers, and toothpicks to make my still life three-dimensional because I didn't think I could make the bird look as alive if I just drew or painted it. I attached it to construction paper facing east because the sun rises in the east and this stanza happens at dawn.

Still warming my fingers
round a cup, *café* I made
in the quiet
before the world fills the air.

Artist Statement for Stanza Two:
Christina

My still life was made with clay, pipe cleaners, and acrylic paint on brown construction paper. I chose brown paper because I wanted it to look like coffee, and the cup comes out from the paper because I wanted people to feel like they could touch it like the speaker does, "Still warming my fingers / round a cup." As you can see, the world just slightly comes into the picture. This is foreshadowing since the world hasn't filled the air yet in this stanza. I wanted the world to be kind of big though, not just off in the corner, because I have a feeling that once it takes over nothing will be quiet.

Still opening these doors
heavier now
with my own hands,
weathered brown on brown.

Artist Statement for Stanza Three:
Kevin

The line I liked most in this stanza was the last one, "weathered brown on brown," so I decided to show how the hand and the door are both weathered. Ms. Wood brought in a bunch of scrap metal and leaves from outside, and I found the perfect piece of metal. It was almost the same color as the leaves and it really was heavy. It was hard to make a hand out of crunched up leaves, but I wanted it to look as weathered as possible. I drew some glue in the shape of a hand and made it look like it was reaching out to open the door.

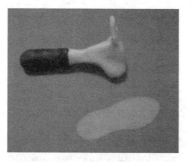

Still holding soles and hammer
mending leather stubborn as my palms
        gently drumming
        gently drumming.

Artist Statement for Stanza Four:
Scott

For stanza four, I made a hammer out of Model Magic and the sole of a shoe out of construction paper. I put the hammer above the sole to show that it is "gently drumming" on the sole. I didn't want to include anything that could move like "my palms" because a still life isn't supposed to have movement. I just wanted to show what was being held.

Still sweeping slowly as the sun
sets before I walk to the *plaza*
to watch the stars come out,
to watch the girls.

Spring again.

Artist Statement for Stanza Five:
Veronica

I thought that it would be interesting to create a still life of what the room looked like after the speaker left to go to the plaza. The broom is left alone in the corner, and you can see the stars through the window. I knew that the broom had to be part of my picture because that's what the speaker is still doing before the stars come out. I used clay and toothpicks to make the broom, and I used Popsicle sticks, toothpicks, Model Magic, and a black marker to make the window.

Classroom Snapshot: While my students worked on this project, I noticed that they were learning to pay attention to detail without much prompting. My goal was for them to see the poem in new ways through their artwork, and by focusing in on single images, they were able to make the kinds of connections that they had missed when studying other poems. For example, several students noticed that Pat Mora mentions hands in three of the six stanzas in this poem. This led to a discussion of the different reasons Mora might have repeated this image. The ideas they came up with are as follows:

- The speaker is trying to describe herself/himself by showing what the hands do. The hands are weathered and stubborn and need to be kept warm.

- Hands are used as tools to open doors and mend soles in this poem so maybe Mora is saying that the hands are the most important part of the speaker.

- This poem is about showing pieces of the speaker's day or life through specific images. Pat Mora might have decided that she needed to focus up close on one part of the speaker instead of showing everything.

Students were able to interpret this poem using detailed examples from the text so this project became more than just an exercise in converting words to images. It enabled students to work closely with a poem to create something of their own and to more effectively use textual evidence to defend their points of view.

Extension

Writing from National Geographic *Photos*

The photographs found in *National Geographic* magazine are exceptional tools to get students to write from images. Play a game by spreading a pile of *National Geographic* photos on a table and letting students choose one. Tell them that their task is to tell a story about the picture or describe the picture in detail without giving away its contents. Then, pick up all the pictures and redistribute them, making sure that everyone has a new photo. Now pick up the descriptions that the students wrote and read the first one aloud. As soon as someone thinks they have the picture that goes with the description, they should stand up and yell "Bingo!" Whoever guesses correctly gets to read the next description unless they don't want to or the handwriting is too illegible. The game continues this way until all the pictures have been matched up with their descriptions. This is a great way to share students' work without requiring that they read it in front of everyone.

5 Where to Go When You Can't Get Enough

The following list is by no means exhaustive but is meant to serve as a resource for teachers who want to find out more about the poets in this book, their work, or the teaching of poetry. I chose to include as many books related to Giovanni, Lee, and Mora as I possibly could, keeping their relevance in mind. While there are many other books on the market that have to do with the teaching of poetry, I decided to include only those that have made the most difference to my colleagues and me in the "Teaching Poetry" section of this chapter.

I recommend investing in the individual collections of poetry listed below to add to your classroom's library. This will provide students with additional works by these authors that are readily available, and it will allow you to include new poems to your curriculum that may coincide well with the poetry presented in *Living Voices*.

The first three sections below begin with a list of these individual collections followed by other works by each author. The last two sections include poetry anthologies and several resources for teaching poetry. After the lists of individual collections, each citation includes a brief annotation describing the book and how it may be useful to you and/or your students.

Nikki Giovanni

Giovanni, Nikki. *Black Feeling, Black Talk, Black Judgement*. New York: William Morrow, 1971.

Giovanni, Nikki. *Blues: For All the Changes*. New York: William Morrow, 1999.

Giovanni, Nikki. *Cotton Candy on a Rainy Day*. New York: William Morrow, 1978.

Giovanni, Nikki. *Ego Tripping and Other Poems for Young People*. Chicago: Lawrence Hill, 1993.

Giovanni, Nikki. *Love Poems*. New York: William Morrow, 1997.

Giovanni, Nikki. *My House*. New York: Perennial, 1974.

Giovanni, Nikki. *Quilting the Black-Eyed Pea: Poems and Not Quite Poems*. New York: William Morrow, 2002.

Giovanni, Nikki. *Re: Creation*. Detroit: Broadside Press, 1970.

Giovanni, Nikki. *Those Who Ride the Night Winds*. New York: William Morrow, 1983.

Giovanni, Nikki. *The Women and the Men*. New York: William Morrow, 1979.

Giovanni, Nikki. *Gemini, An Extended Statement on My First Twenty-Five Years of Being a Black Poet*. New York: Viking Press, 1976.

This phenomenal collection of autobiographical essays is a record of Giovanni's early life as a writer and black woman during the 1960s. The essays are both personal and socially insightful. Written in the same welcoming language that is found in her poetry, students will have no problem diving into them. Since this autobiography is broken up into a series of essays, it is easy for teachers and students to take one essay to use in the classroom or to read the entire collection.

Giovanni, Nikki. *Racism 101*. New York: William Morrow, 1994.

In this collection of essays, Giovanni shares wisdom on the difficulties of being a black student on a predominantly white college campus. In true Nikki Giovanni style, these essays are frankly honest and genuinely caring. She uncovers the many inequalities on college campuses and exposes the racism that tries to hide there and in society. Many of these essays could be used in English and social studies classrooms to illustrate the battles that continue today for people of color in the United States.

Giovanni, Nikki. *Sacred Cows and Other Edibles*. New York: Quill, 1989.

Giovanni expresses her strong attitudes about everything under the sun— from insects to poverty, prejudice to television commercials—in this collection of essays. Giovanni doesn't hold back when it comes to expressing her opinions, which students will appreciate. This collection is funny, insightful, and soulful. These essays are wonderful examples of voice and humor in nonfiction writing, and therefore would serve as effective models for students.

Giovanni, Nikki. *The Selected Poems of Nikki Giovanni*. New York: William Morrow, 1997.

This collection includes poetry from the previously published *Black Feeling, Black Talk, Black Judgement*, published in 1971, to *Those Who Ride the Night Winds*, first published in 1983, with several poems appearing for the first time in this compilation. All of the poems used in *Living Voices* can be found in *The Selected Poems of Nikki Giovanni*, which also includes a detailed chronology of Nikki Giovanni's life. Owning this compilation is an easy way to keep most of Giovanni's poetry in one place. This is a volume that you might want to keep with your other reference books.

Nikki Giovanni's Web site can be found at www.nikki-giovanni. com. It includes a biography, poetry, recordings of her reading some of her work, lists of her books and other publications, awards, etc. This site will tell you just about anything you would want to know about Nikki Giovanni.

Li-Young Lee

Lee, Li-Young. *Book of My Nights: Poems*. New York: BOA Editions, 2001.

Lee, Li-Young. *The City in Which I Love You*. New York: BOA Editions, 1990.

Lee, Li-Young. *Rose*. New York: BOA Editions, 1986.

Lee, Li-Young. *The Winged Seed: A Remembrance*. New York: Simon & Schuster, 1995.

This amazing memoir does not just give an account of Lee's life but of the history of his family and his people. He speaks of China, Indonesia (where he was born), Hong Kong, and finally America, where his family settled. Lee is objective about most events while weaving the perception of childhood in and out of his stories using the haunting language that pervades much of his poetry. Students and teachers alike will gain valuable insight into the mind of Li-Young Lee from studying his life, which will make for a much richer poetry-reading experience.

Pat Mora

Mora, Pat. *Agua Santa: Holy Water*. Boston: Beacon Press, 1995.

Mora, Pat. *Aunt Carmen's Book of Practical Saints*. Boston: Beacon Press, 1997.

Mora, Pat. *Borders*. Houston: Arte Público Press, 1986.

Mora, Pat. *Chants*. Houston: Arte Público Press, 1984.

Mora, Pat. *Communion*. Houston: Arte Público Press, 1991.

Mora, Pat. *My Own True Name: New and Selected Poems for Young Adults*. Houston: Arte Público Press, 2000.

Mora, Pat. *House of Houses*. Boston: Beacon Press, 1997.

> When students want to know more about an author, it is best to send them right to the source. Mora's life story is written like a novel, making it easily accessible to most students. They are not only able to grasp it, but they can relate to it personally.

Mora, Pat. *Nepantla: Essays from the Land in the Middle*. Albuquerque: U of New Mexico P, 1993.

> In this poignant collection of essays, Mora explores what it means to be Latina in the United States. Like the nonfiction writing of Giovanni and Lee, this book would serve well as a resource in the English or the social studies classroom.

Pat Mora's Web site can be found at www.patmora.com. This site is full of resources for teachers and students including curriculum extensions, resources for serving Latino children and families, letters from Pat to students, and an extensive bibliography of articles on Pat's writing for adults and children. This site also lists all of Pat Mora's publications, biographical information, and ways to contact her.

Poetry Anthologies

Brewbaker, James, and Dawnelle J. Hyland, eds. *Poems by Adolescents and Adults: A Thematic Collection for Middle School and High School*. Urbana: NCTE, 2002.

> Most collections of poetry include work by well-established poets who have spent years proving themselves to the rest of the poetry world, but this anthology is different in that it combines work from famous writers like Nikki Giovanni with classroom teachers and students in grades 5 to 12. Organized in themes such as peer pressure, love, and life in the future, this anthology is incredibly accessible for students to pick up on their own or to study as part of classroom instruction.

Gillan, Maria Mazziotti, and Jennifer Gillan, eds. *Unsettling America: An Anthology of Contemporary Multicultural Poetry*. New York: Penguin, 1994.

This anthology is a wonderful addition to any poetry library. Giovanni, Lee, and Mora are all included, as well as dozens of other inspirational poets such as Yusef Komunyakaa, Naomi Shihab Nye, and Jimmy Santiago Baca. Not only are all of the voices in this anthology living, but they also all have diverse cultural backgrounds. When you have exhausted the poetry of Giovanni, Lee, and Mora, there are still other poets left to be discovered. Show students that poetry is not a dead art form. There are dozens of poets in this book that can do just that.

Greenberg, Jan, ed. *Heart to Heart: New Poems Inspired by 20th Century American Art*. New York: Harry N. Abrams, 2001.

For this anthology, poets such as Joy Harjo and Gary Gildner were commissioned to write poems inspired by contemporary artwork by artists ranging from Georgia O'Keeffe to Andy Warhol. Besides being a beautiful picture book, this collection will be a useful tool for any teacher who wants to incorporate art and poetry into their classroom.

Hopkins, Lee Bennett, ed. *Hand in Hand: An American History Through Poetry*. New York: Simon & Schuster, 1994.

An amazing group of poets is compiled in this anthology to tell the story of America's history from the time the first pilgrims landed on our eastern shores to the Vietnam War and beyond. Skillfully illustrated with watercolor paintings, this book is a good example of different poetic forms and various ways poetry can describe our historical landscape.

Janeczko, Paul B., ed. *Wherever Home Begins: 100 Contemporary Poems*. New York: Orchard Books, 1995.

I decided to include this anthology because of the possibilities it allows for interdisciplinary study using the poems included in the anthology. While reading this anthology, I was swept from New York City to South Dakota to "An English Garden in Autumn" in a poem by Christine E. Hemp. These poems also take readers to places of historical and cultural importance such as Anne Frank's house in Amsterdam and a border town in Arizona. This anthology will bring poetry to life in geography and history classes just as it will bring a strong sense of place to language arts lessons.

Nye, Naomi Shihab, and Paul B. Janeczko, eds. *I Feel a Little Jumpy Around You: A Book of Her Poems and His Poems Collected in Pairs*. New York: Simon Pulse, 1996.

> This award-winning anthology is full of contemporary poetry arranged in female/male duets. A total of 196 poems have been paired together to demonstrate the different and similar ways in which men and women think and write about the same topics. Edited by two renowned poets, this collection includes some of our most prized living voices, many of whom are from diverse ethnic and cultural backgrounds.

Philip, Neil, ed. *Singing America: Poems that Define a Nation*. New York: Viking, 1995.

> While this anthology is somewhat like *Hand in Hand*, it is unique in that it contains a more diverse collection of poetry and its focus is as much on place as it is on the story of our nation. A myriad of American voices such as immigrants, miners, African Americans, and Native Americans are celebrated here. This is another book that should be part of every history class.

Teaching Poetry

Behn, Robin, and Chase Twichell, eds. *The Practice of Poetry: Writing Exercises From Poets Who Teach*. New York: Harper Resource, 1992.

> What better way to study poetry than by learning from poets firsthand? This guide includes ninety writing exercises by an assortment of poets who teach. I came across this book while looking for ways to jump start my own writing and was left with dozens of ideas to try in the classroom. While some of the lessons in this book are rather sophisticated in their language and goals for students, I have found that most of the instructions can be easily adapted for students of all ages and ability levels, and once again, most of the poets included in this book are living and teaching right here in America.

Dunning, Stephen, and William Stafford. *Getting the Knack: 20 Poetry Writing Exercises*. Urbana: NCTE, 1992.

> While this book was written for any novice poet, it serves as an effective teaching tool in the classroom. The authors, who are poets themselves, write in a conversational style that welcomes readers to interact. They have included forms of poetry that are sometimes forgotten about in the classroom such as found or

headline poems and letter poems. Each chapter contains a step-by-step guide to writing poetry that can easily be adapted for the middle school classroom.

Jago, Carol. *Nikki Giovanni in the Classroom: "The same ol danger but a brand new pleasure."* Urbana: NCTE, 1999.

This book is the first in the National Council of Teachers of English (NCTE) High School Literacy Series. It features several practical lessons along with student work and many of Giovanni's poems printed in full. Jago takes the readers in her high school classroom and shows us firsthand how she uses Giovanni's poetry. While they are meant to be used at the high school level, the lessons in this book will definitely speak to middle school students as well. Other books by Jago in the series include *Alice Walker in the Classroom: "Living by the Word"* and *Sandra Cisneros in the Classroom: "Do not forget to reach."* They can all be found on the NCTE Web site: www.ncte.org.

Koch, Kenneth. *Rose, Where Did You Get That Red? Teaching Great Poems to Children.* New York: Vintage, 1990.

Besides being a fantastic poet, Kenneth Koch has proven himself to be an exceptional teacher of poetry. In this collection, Koch takes poetry that might ordinarily seem to be inaccessible for young readers, such as Rimbaud and Shakespeare, and explains how he taught it to students in exciting, relevant ways. This book contains ten lessons along with student work and an anthology of poetry that includes many greats such as Dickinson, Rilke, and Yeats. It is appropriate for most ages, including adults.

Koch, Kenneth. *Wishes, Lies, and Dreams: Teaching Children to Write Poetry.* New York: Perennial, 1999.

Just before the first edition of this book was published in 1970, Kenneth Koch spent several months teaching elementary school children how to write poetry in Manhattan. *Wishes, Lies, and Dreams* is the result of that experience. His goal was to engage students in writing using the same kind of uninhibited vigor with which they produced artwork. The outcome was phenomenal. Koch not only motivated his students to become confident poets, but teachers all over the country continue to use this text across grade levels to inspire their own students.

Lies, Betty Bonham. *The Poet's Pen: Writing Poetry with Middle and High School Students.* Englewood, CO: Teacher Ideas Press, 1993.

This is a resource that teachers will want to keep with them at their desks. *The Poet's Pen* includes countless ideas to help students start writing poetry, and it explains how to start a poetry writing program in your classroom. Lies focuses on everything from technical details to the nuances of revision, and she explains how poetry can be used as part of an interdisciplinary curriculum. This book also includes exercises and student examples.

Moon, Brian. *Studying Poetry: Activities, Resources, and Texts*. Urbana: NCTE, 2001.

This bestselling teaching resource is an anthology of poetry that incorporates activities ranging from performance to a step-by-step guide to writing about poetry. It is comprised of more than seventy-five poems printed in full text that span from Shakespeare to Plath to Levertov. Moon has also included student writing and teacher comments.

Somers, Albert B. *Teaching Poetry in High School*. Urbana: NCTE, 1999.

This text covers a wide range of issues including assessment, how to use poetry across the curriculum, and poetry on the Internet. It responds to the questions of what kinds of poetry should be taught and what students should know about poetry by the time they are in high school. Somers includes multiple activities that are easily applied and adapted to most classrooms. This book is all about discovering the joys of teaching and understanding poetry.

Tsujimoto, Joseph I. *Teaching Poetry Writing to Adolescents*. Urbana: NCTE, 1988.

As Tsujimoto states in the preface of this book, its purpose "is to serve as a general model for the teaching of poetry writing" (xiii). Much of Tsujimoto's commentary reads like a good novel, ornamented with anecdotes that lead seamlessly into teaching models and extensive student examples. This book includes instruction for how to write, revise, and evaluate using eighteen different writing assignments. It is aimed at junior high students but can be easily adapted for any level.

Appendix

Identifying the Speaker

Directions: In the middle column answer the questions about the speakers. Use the right column to give evidence from the poem to support your answer.

Questions	Answers	Textual Evidence
Are the speakers male or female? "Habits"		
"Choices"		
What activities do these speakers participate in? "Habits"		
"Choices"		
How old are they? "Habits"		
"Choices"		
How do they feel in these poems? "Habits"		
"Choices"		
What from the poems relates to you? "Habits"		
"Choices"		

Living Voices: Multicultural Poetry in the Middle School Classroom by Jaime R. Wood
© 2006 NCTE.

Identifying the Speaker

Directions: Use the Venn diagram to compare and contrast what you know about the speakers from the poems "Habits" and "Choices" and what you know about Nikki Giovanni.

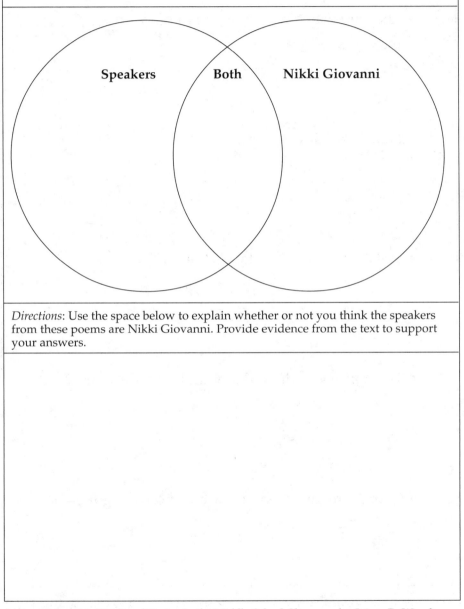

Speakers   **Both**   **Nikki Giovanni**

Directions: Use the space below to explain whether or not you think the speakers from these poems are Nikki Giovanni. Provide evidence from the text to support your answers.

Writing Similes

- They are watching. (How are they watching?)

- I am sick. (How sick are you?)

- The car is fast. (How fast is the car?)

- The house was dark. (How dark was the house?)

- Chores are forgotten. (How are chores forgotten?)

Living Voices: Multicultural Poetry in the Middle School Classroom by Jaime R. Wood
© 2006 NCTE.

The Symbolic World

Directions: Use the left column to list five objects from your daily life that have symbolic meaning. In the middle column, briefly describe what the object is literally. Explain what the object means symbolically in the right column.

Object	Literal Meaning	Symbolic Meaning

Directions: Use the space below to record all of the things in the poem "The Rose Bush" that have symbolic meaning.

Object	Literal Meaning	Symbolic Meaning

Directions: Use the space below to explain what you think the poem "The Rose Bush" means. Use textual evidence and the notes above about the symbolism in the poem to support your answer.

Living Voices: Multicultural Poetry in the Middle School Classroom by Jaime R. Wood © 2006 NCTE.

Language Match

Directions: Match the word in the left column with the description or synonym from the poem. Write the description/synonym in the right column.

Word	Description/Synonym
rice	
boiling	
fire	
morning	
combs (verb form)	
thick	
sound	
fifty	
hair	

Living Voices: Multicultural Poetry in the Middle School Classroom by Jaime R. Wood © 2006 NCTE.

Bio Web

Directions: List the objects from your bio bag in the scroll in the middle of the page. In each numbered circle, write two metaphors for the object that goes with that number.

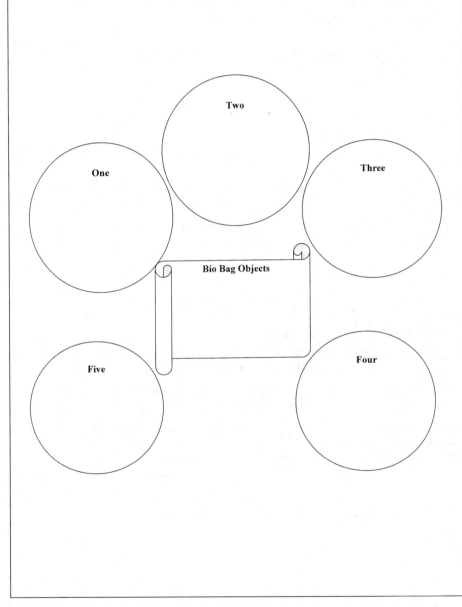

Metaphorical Meaning

Directions: List three important objects from the poem in the left column, what the object was compared with in the middle column, and a brief explanation for each answer in the right column. The explanation column might describe how the metaphor helps the reader understand the meaning of the poem. (You may need more space to write the explanations. Use the back of this sheet or a separate piece of paper if necessary.)

Object	Metaphor	Explanation

Synthesizing Meaning

Directions: Read the following questions carefully and use the space below to record your answers. Please answer the questions in complete sentences and include examples from the poem to support your answers.
- Why do you think this memory was important enough for Lee to write a poem about it?
- What might this memory represent?
- What from the poem makes you believe this?

Name_____

You're a Character

Directions: List three characteristics about your partner in each box.

Internal	External
Thoughts	Personality
1.	1.
2.	2.
3.	3.
Emotions	Physical
1.	1.
2.	2.
3.	3.

Living Voices: Multicultural Poetry in the Middle School Classroom by Jaime R. Wood
© 2006 NCTE.

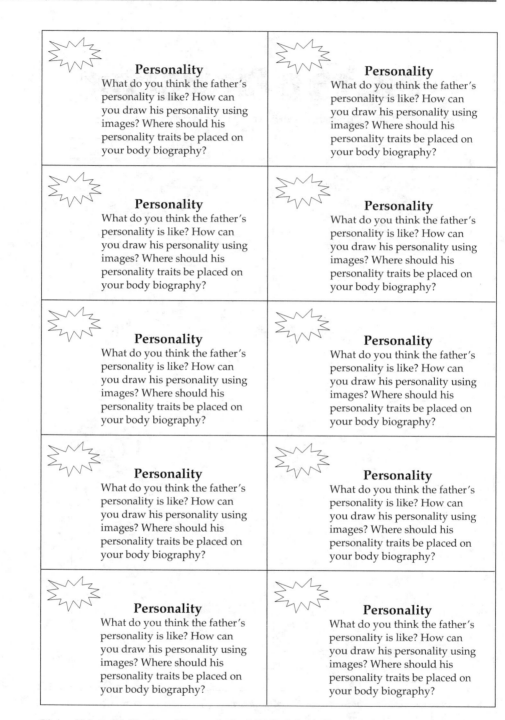

Personality
What do you think the father's personality is like? How can you draw his personality using images? Where should his personality traits be placed on your body biography?

Personality
What do you think the father's personality is like? How can you draw his personality using images? Where should his personality traits be placed on your body biography?

Personality
What do you think the father's personality is like? How can you draw his personality using images? Where should his personality traits be placed on your body biography?

Personality
What do you think the father's personality is like? How can you draw his personality using images? Where should his personality traits be placed on your body biography?

Personality
What do you think the father's personality is like? How can you draw his personality using images? Where should his personality traits be placed on your body biography?

Personality
What do you think the father's personality is like? How can you draw his personality using images? Where should his personality traits be placed on your body biography?

Personality
What do you think the father's personality is like? How can you draw his personality using images? Where should his personality traits be placed on your body biography?

Personality
What do you think the father's personality is like? How can you draw his personality using images? Where should his personality traits be placed on your body biography?

Personality
What do you think the father's personality is like? How can you draw his personality using images? Where should his personality traits be placed on your body biography?

Personality
What do you think the father's personality is like? How can you draw his personality using images? Where should his personality traits be placed on your body biography?

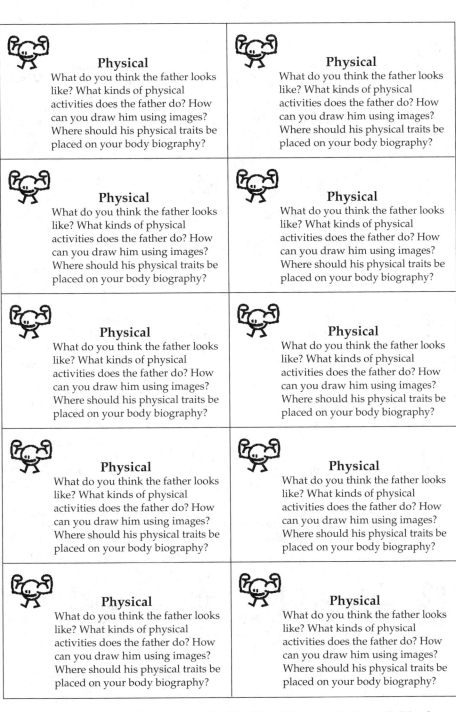

Physical
What do you think the father looks like? What kinds of physical activities does the father do? How can you draw him using images? Where should his physical traits be placed on your body biography?

Physical
What do you think the father looks like? What kinds of physical activities does the father do? How can you draw him using images? Where should his physical traits be placed on your body biography?

Physical
What do you think the father looks like? What kinds of physical activities does the father do? How can you draw him using images? Where should his physical traits be placed on your body biography?

Physical
What do you think the father looks like? What kinds of physical activities does the father do? How can you draw him using images? Where should his physical traits be placed on your body biography?

Physical
What do you think the father looks like? What kinds of physical activities does the father do? How can you draw him using images? Where should his physical traits be placed on your body biography?

Physical
What do you think the father looks like? What kinds of physical activities does the father do? How can you draw him using images? Where should his physical traits be placed on your body biography?

Physical
What do you think the father looks like? What kinds of physical activities does the father do? How can you draw him using images? Where should his physical traits be placed on your body biography?

Physical
What do you think the father looks like? What kinds of physical activities does the father do? How can you draw him using images? Where should his physical traits be placed on your body biography?

Physical
What do you think the father looks like? What kinds of physical activities does the father do? How can you draw him using images? Where should his physical traits be placed on your body biography?

Physical
What do you think the father looks like? What kinds of physical activities does the father do? How can you draw him using images? Where should his physical traits be placed on your body biography?

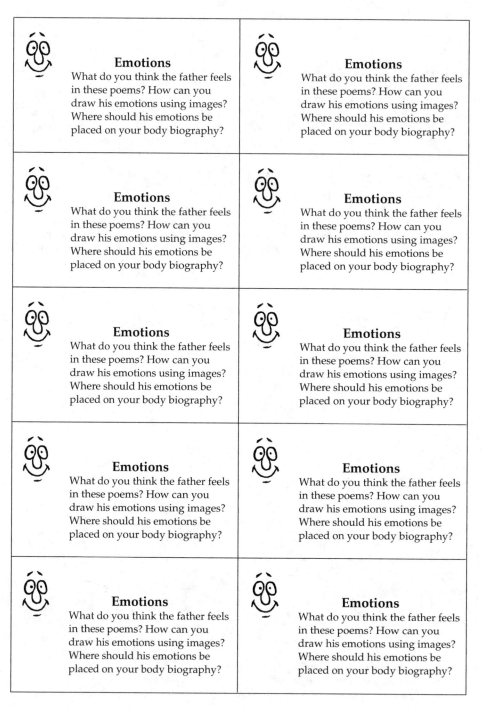

Emotions
What do you think the father feels in these poems? How can you draw his emotions using images? Where should his emotions be placed on your body biography?

Emotions
What do you think the father feels in these poems? How can you draw his emotions using images? Where should his emotions be placed on your body biography?

Emotions
What do you think the father feels in these poems? How can you draw his emotions using images? Where should his emotions be placed on your body biography?

Emotions
What do you think the father feels in these poems? How can you draw his emotions using images? Where should his emotions be placed on your body biography?

Emotions
What do you think the father feels in these poems? How can you draw his emotions using images? Where should his emotions be placed on your body biography?

Emotions
What do you think the father feels in these poems? How can you draw his emotions using images? Where should his emotions be placed on your body biography?

Emotions
What do you think the father feels in these poems? How can you draw his emotions using images? Where should his emotions be placed on your body biography?

Emotions
What do you think the father feels in these poems? How can you draw his emotions using images? Where should his emotions be placed on your body biography?

Emotions
What do you think the father feels in these poems? How can you draw his emotions using images? Where should his emotions be placed on your body biography?

Emotions
What do you think the father feels in these poems? How can you draw his emotions using images? Where should his emotions be placed on your body biography?

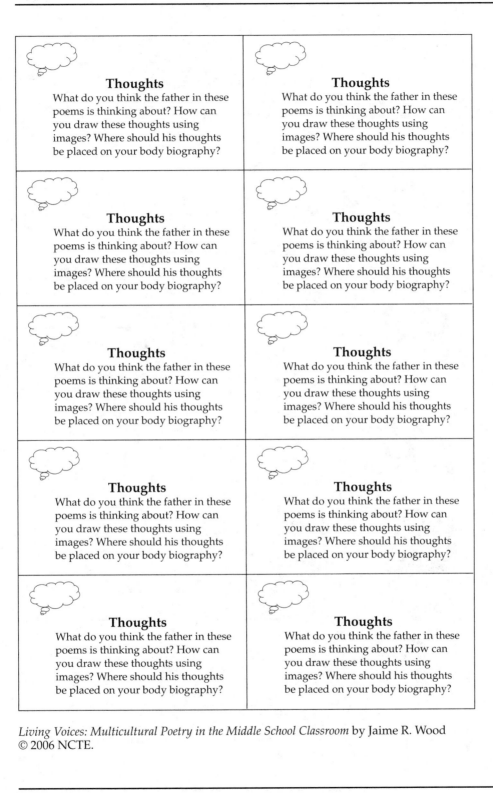

Thoughts
What do you think the father in these poems is thinking about? How can you draw these thoughts using images? Where should his thoughts be placed on your body biography?

Thoughts
What do you think the father in these poems is thinking about? How can you draw these thoughts using images? Where should his thoughts be placed on your body biography?

Thoughts
What do you think the father in these poems is thinking about? How can you draw these thoughts using images? Where should his thoughts be placed on your body biography?

Thoughts
What do you think the father in these poems is thinking about? How can you draw these thoughts using images? Where should his thoughts be placed on your body biography?

Thoughts
What do you think the father in these poems is thinking about? How can you draw these thoughts using images? Where should his thoughts be placed on your body biography?

Thoughts
What do you think the father in these poems is thinking about? How can you draw these thoughts using images? Where should his thoughts be placed on your body biography?

Thoughts
What do you think the father in these poems is thinking about? How can you draw these thoughts using images? Where should his thoughts be placed on your body biography?

Thoughts
What do you think the father in these poems is thinking about? How can you draw these thoughts using images? Where should his thoughts be placed on your body biography?

Thoughts
What do you think the father in these poems is thinking about? How can you draw these thoughts using images? Where should his thoughts be placed on your body biography?

Thoughts
What do you think the father in these poems is thinking about? How can you draw these thoughts using images? Where should his thoughts be placed on your body biography?

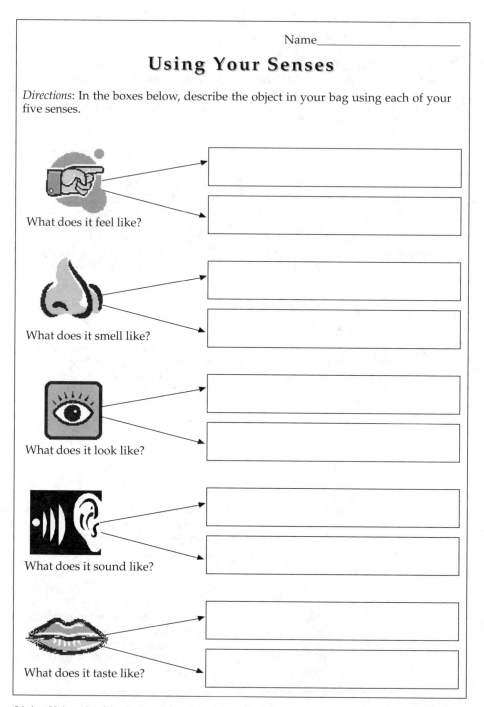

Name_____

Using Your Senses

Directions: In the boxes below, describe the object in your bag using each of your five senses.

What does it feel like?

What does it smell like?

What does it look like?

What does it sound like?

What does it taste like?

Living Voices: Multicultural Poetry in the Middle School Classroom by Jaime R. Wood
© 2006 NCTE.

A Personification Riddle

His hands twist around
before I can catch them,
stop them from turning me old,
always in circles he runs
with my years, hiding memories
behind the *tick tick ticking*
of his brain, red tongue mocking
me as I try to keep up.

What object did I personify?
A clock.

Name_____

Personification

Directions: In the left column, list three human characteristics from each poem. In the right column, compare the human characteristics with the object being described (desert or moon). Use complete sentences in the right column.

"Mi Madre"	
Human Characteristics	Compared to the desert
Example: "She serves red prickly pears on a spiked cactus."	The desert "serves" prickly pears by providing the soil for cactus to grow the prickly pears.

"Luna, Luna"	
Human Characteristics	Compared to the moon

Directions: In complete sentences, explain why you think Pat Mora decided to personify the desert and the moon in these poems. Use textual evidence to explain your answer.

Living Voices: Multicultural Poetry in the Middle School Classroom by Jaime R. Wood
© 2006 NCTE.

I Have a Dream

Directions: Use the space below to write your section of the speech. This will help you become more familiar with the speech and will make the speech easily accessible while you define the words and phrases from your section.

Directions: Use the space below to record information about the words and/or phrases from your section of the speech. List the words and/or phrases in the left column, record the meanings you found through research in the middle column, and explain what the words and/or phrases mean in the context of Martin Luther King Jr.'s speech in the right column.

Word/Phrase from Speech	Definition	Meaning in Context

Directions: Use the space below to write a paragraph explaining what your section of the speech is saying. Explain it so that your classmates will have a clearer idea of what the speech means when you share your paragraph.

Brain Questions

- What are the three different types of memory?

- Which parts of the brain are responsible for each type of memory?

- What are some problems with memory?

- What are mnemonic devices?

- Why do mnemonic devices work?

Name_____

Framing the World

Directions: Use the space below to draw everything inside your frame to the best of your ability paying close attention to details.

Directions: Write a detailed description of what is inside your frame as if you are trying to describe it to someone who has never seen it before. Be sure to use all of your senses to create as vivid a picture as possible.

Works Cited

Beck, Emily Morison, ed. *Familiar Quotations: A Collection of Passages, Phrases, and Proverbs Traced to Their Sources in Ancient and Modern Literature.* Boston: Little, Brown, 1968.

Bloom, Benjamin S. *Taxonomy of Educational Objectives.* Boston: Allyn and Bacon, 1984.

Exploratorium. "Memory." 1998-1999. 22 Dec. 2004 <http://www.exploratorium.edu/memory/>.

Giovanni, Nikki. *Black Feeling, Black Talk, Black Judgement.* New York: William Morrow, 1970.

Giovanni, Nikki. *Cotton Candy on a Rainy Day.* New York: Quill, 1980.

Giovanni, Nikki. "Nikki Giovanni Timeline." 2002, 2003. 15 Nov. 2003 <http://69.65.21.121/~nikkigi/timeline.shtml>.

Giovanni, Nikki. *The Selected Poems of Nikki Giovanni.* New York: William Morrow, 1996.

Justice, Donald. "Poem to be Read at 3 A.M." *Night Light.* Middletown, CT: Wesleyan UP, 1981.

King, Martin Luther, Jr. "I Have a Dream." 2001-2005 3 June 2005 <http://www.americanrhetoric.com/speeches/Ihaveadream.htm>.

King, Martin Luther. "I See the Promised Land (3 April 1968)." *A Testament of Hope: The Essential Writings and Speeches of Martin Luther King, Jr.* Ed. James M. Washington. New York: HarperCollins, 1991. 279.

King, Martin Luther. "Letter from Birmingham City Jail (1963)." *A Testament of Hope: The Essential Writings and Speeches of Martin Luther King, Jr.* Ed. James M. Washington. New York: HarperCollins, 1991. 289.

Lee, Li-Young. *Rose.* Brockport, New York: BOA Editions, 1986.

Lee, Li-Young. "Words for Worry." *Book of My Nights.* New York: BOA Editions, 2001.

Mora, Pat. *Borders.* Houston: Arte Publico Press, 1986.

Mora, Pat. *Chants.* Houston: Arte Publico Press, 1984.

Mora, Pat. *Communion.* Houston: Arte Publico Press, 1991.

Pent, Michael. "Manzanilla as Medicine." 10 Mar. 2005 <http://www.abroadviewmagazine.com/regions/lat_amer/manz_med.html>.

Rich, Adrienne. "Invisibility in Academe." *Blood, Bread, and Poetry: Selected Prose: 1979-1985.* New York: Norton, 1994.

Underwood, William. "The Body Biography: A Framework for Student Writing." *English Journal* 76 (1987): 44–48.

Author

Photo by Stephanie G'Schwind

Jaime R. Wood has been working with school-age children for close to ten years in different capacities, but much of her formal teaching experience has come from Pioneer School for Expeditionary Learning, the first expeditionary-learning outward-bound school in northern Colorado, which she helped start in 2001. Her experience at Pioneer School provided the foundation for what she has created in *Living Voices*. After teaching at Pioneer, Jaime taught composition at Colorado State University for two years while finishing her master's degree in English education. She is currently relocating to Austin, Texas, with her cats Felicity and Monte.

This book was typeset in Palatino and Helvetica by Electronic Imaging.
Typefaces used on the cover were Fashion Compressed and Copperplate Gothic.
The book was printed on 50-lb. Williamsburg Offset paper by Versa Press, Inc.